To those who fought for our community, thank you.

To those who are just coming into our community, welcome.

Let's get you caught up.

RAINBOW

YOUR GUIDE THROUGH
QUEER AND TRANS HISTORY

HISTORY
CLASS

HANNAH McELHINNEY

Hardie Grant

BOOKS

Welcome to Class   4

CHAPTER ONE
The Ancient World   8

CHAPTER TWO
The Queer Estatic   36

CHAPTER THREE
God, Gold and Glory   56

CHAPTER FOUR
Have You Heard the   74
Rumours?

CHAPTER FIVE
Through Science to   86
Justice

CHAPTER SIX
Welcome to the Secret   98
Society

CHAPTER SEVEN

Meanwhile, in Hollywood 112

CHAPTER EIGHT

Nothing's Fair in Love and War 124

CHAPTER NINE

Darling, I Want My Gay Rights Now 138

CHAPTER TEN

It's In Vogue 158

CHAPTER ELEVEN

Silence = Death 168

CHAPTER TWELVE

The Internet is the New Gay Bar 188

An Army of Lovers Cannot Lose 206
Further Reading 208
Acknowledgements 211
Index 213

Welcome to Class

In 371 BCE, the Theban army spectacularly defeated the Spartans in the Battle of Leuctra. Their secret? An elite unit comprised of 150 pairs of male lovers. This elite unit was named the Sacred Band of Thebes and it was formed after an Ancient Greek philosopher argued that an army of lovers could defeat the entire world. The idea was that a man in love would sooner die a thousand deaths than have his lover see him as a coward. Love, too, meant the pairs would stop at nothing to protect each other. All this considered, the Spartans never had a chance.

The Sacred Band of Thebes was eventually disbanded, but the idea that an army of queer lovers could defeat almost any enemy recurs like a heartbeat throughout history. During the Golden Age of Piracy, pirates fought valiantly side by side with their same-sex lovers, pledging, as pirates do, to go to hell together. Marches, protests and uprisings – what are they if not an army of lovers fighting against the enemy of oppression? This same idea can be found in the lesbian feminist poetry of the 70s, the urgent radical queer zines of the 90s, and in the hashtag movements that crash through the internet today. The idea that an army of lovers can't lose has bound us together through time and space as we have fought for our freedom as queer people, as trans people.

After the Sacred Band of Thebes, no other military body has really considered queer or trans people to be particularly strong, which is a huge oversight. In fact, as you'll read in Chapter 8 of this book, the military went to a lot of effort to keep us *out* of their ranks. But the army of lovers we're focussed on is less a military division and more of a resistance. One that spans time and place and manifests in fashion, language, relationships, art, music, neighbourhoods, spirituality, and a refusal to accept the dominant constructs of gender and sexuality that have been thrust upon us.

As you read on, you'll meet a varied group of individuals who fought as part of this army. Some fought with weapons (or, as you'll discover, a bucket of sheep's brains), some fought with words, and some fought simply by being themselves when society had other plans.

Before we get into it, here's a quick note on some of the terminology you'll come across in these pages. We've chosen to use the words queer and transgender (and trans for short) as umbrella terms that encompass all sexualities and genders that defy society's rather rigid rules. These terms feel the closest to what we want to express, but we do acknowledge that 'queer' was once a harmful slur and there are people in our community who will still have the flinch of this word in their muscle memory.

Then there's the acronym. You'll see it grow and evolve over the course of the book; however, when we are referring to our community as a whole, we have used LGBTQ+. The acronym looks different in different countries and communities, so we've chosen a version that feels the most broad.

It's a careful dance using these words to describe long-dead people because our modern constructs of gender and sexuality didn't apply in other time periods. Then again, for the most part, historical figures have been assumed to be cisgender or heterosexual without much interrogation. What's up with that?

The way history is presented says as much about the person *telling* the story and the time in which it was told as it does about the people and times that feature in it. We often see history as a great never-ending story, but in actuality it's more of a grand mess. As humans, we love to fashion what is essentially a sprawling nebula of events into a tidy three-act narrative with a few charismatic main characters. We pull out certain details and assign them importance while ignoring those we don't feel are relevant or that might even interfere with the palatable story we're trying to tell.

We have missed out on so much queer and trans history because it's those in power that get to make all of these narrative decisions.

This is why it's also important to acknowledge that this book has been written from a Western perspective by a white Australian person living on stolen land. The majority of the sources we relied on were in English, meaning they were either written from a Western viewpoint or have been filtered through a Western lens in translation. We also can't assume that images are a source of objective truth; if an image is worth a thousand words, most of them would be written about the photographer. As queer and transgender people have historically been viewed as criminals or curiosities, a great deal of imagery presents them in this way.

In addition, the historical icons we know most about are white gay men. Because homosexuality among men (not women) was illegal for hundreds of years, there are court records revealing its prevalence at different times. If these men were of high social standing a scandal would have ensued, resulting in media coverage or other documentation. People of colour typically weren't afforded this social status in Western society, so their arrests were less documented.

We encourage anybody with access to other languages, sources and experiences to use this book as a starting point to continue their own journey through queer and trans history in other communities and other parts of the world.

The book has been designed to take on you on a journey starting somewhere around the time of the first stone building right up to the time of TikTok. It might be chronological(ish), but it's certainly not linear. There have been periods when diverse genders and sexualities were not just accepted, but celebrated. But these have been followed by periods of extreme persecution and violence. The road we're attempting to carve through time is not straight (nor is anything else in this book, for that matter) but meandering, at times straying into some very dark places.

This book is less about particular milestones, like when same-sex marriage was legalised in different countries, or when trans people were legally allowed to have their true genders reflected on their birth certificates. These are monumental moments that have indeed shaped our history, and they are the fruits of our labour, dreams and rage. They're important. But while these are moments in the stories of governments and societies that affect us, they are not us. Trans women were no less women before it said so on their birth certificates. Same-sex relationships were no less loving before they were officialised by marriage.

We're more interested in how we came to be. What is the story of queerness, of transness, of the historical forces that have shaped our lives, cultures and sense of identity? Our story doesn't exist in a silo, like some kind of subplot in the primary narrative of humanity. Just like everyone who's ever spent time on this planet, we too have been shaped by world wars, empires, religion, disasters, monarchies, economies, science and technology. In that sense, perhaps this isn't a history of queer and trans people, but history as it happened to us.

We hope you find something in here that inspires you, validates you, makes you laugh, brings you gratitude, or at the very least helps you win an argument.

CHAPTER ONE

The Ancient World

Just outside of Cairo lies the site of Saqqara, which houses the necropolis (a kind of elaborate cemetery) for the Ancient Egyptian capital, Memphis. The site is believed to have been the first stone building in the world, finished long before the Pyramids of Giza.

Egyptologists have made numerous discoveries at Saqqara that give us clues about the way humans lived nearly five thousand years ago. However, in 1964 they discovered a tomb that left them baffled. The tomb appeared to be the burial place of two men who, according to the surrounding hieroglyphics, were royal manicurists named Khnumhotep and Niankhkhnum.

For such an elite tomb to be shared by two men of the same rank, rather than a man surrounded by his wife and children, was highly unusual – especially given that both men had wives and children.

Now 1964 wasn't a wonderful year to be homosexual, so naturally scholars concluded the two men may have been twins – even conjoined twins – or brothers, at the very least. And of course, that's perfectly possible. There were no human remains in the tomb, so we have no way of proving (or disproving) a genetic connection. But brothers being buried together (let alone brothers who both had wives) would have been unheard of at the time.

There is, of course, another explanation: that the two men may have been lovers. It speaks volumes that the walls of Khnumhotep and Niankhkhnum's tomb consistently depict the men in positions exclusive to husband and wife – always embracing, and often facing each other with their noses touching, which is the most intimate pose seen in Ancient Egyptian art. The pair are pictured front and centre, with their purported wives appearing in the background in a manner that, according to some historians, suggests acceptance and even approval of the men's relationship.

Historians and scholars have offered many 'explanations' for these 'unusual' finds, and it's impossible to entirely discredit these. But if the tomb of Khnumhotep and Niankhkhnum contained man and woman, there would be no explanation required: their marriage would be assumed. Remember, history is written through the lens and values of the present.

But if we do take the clues presented to us by Khnumhotep and Niankhkhnum, we may very well have documented evidence of same-sex love dating back to the twenty-fifth century BCE.

Artwork in the tomb of Niankhkhnum and Khnumhotep depicts these royal manicurists nose to nose and embracing in a pose usually unique to married couples.

Ancient Egypt is one of the world's oldest civilisations. Artefacts from the time tell us a great deal about life back then, when pharaohs reigned and eyeliner was rightfully important. On top of the evidence we've seen from this tomb, there are other indications that same-sex love and eroticism was common at this time, and even accepted. Ancient texts refer to women sleeping with women, and numerous artworks depict women together with sexual symbolism. In Talmudic literature (ancient texts concerning Jewish law), sex between women was even described as 'the doings of the Land of Egypt'.

That said, this doesn't mean these Ancient Egyptians were homosexual – not in the modern sense. The concept of who you're attracted to forming part of your identity won't emerge for a few thousand years yet.

Hatshepsut

Okay, so there was no concept of sexual identity in ancient times, but gender was definitely a thing, and one of Egypt's most successful pharaohs royally bent it better than anyone.

Hatshepsut was a female pharaoh who reigned from around 1479 to 1458 BCE. Female pharaohs were rare, though not unheard of, but Hatshepsut was unlike any other female pharaoh. She ruled not as queen, but as king.

Hatshepsut was consistently portrayed in a masculine manner, usually with a male body, a beard and in men's clothing. Pharaohs had god-like power in Ancient Egypt, which meant Hatshepsut was in control of how she was viewed (she even designed her own tomb). She used that control to have many feminine depictions of herself changed to masculine ones.

Male dress and false beards were traditional symbols of the Pharaonic Office, so it's possible Hatshepsut wore them to secure her status as a pharaoh, rather than a queen or 'wife of a king'. Many ambitious women throughout history have done the same thing. However, writing from the period suggests Hatshepsut had a more fluid relationship with gender. She used masculine terms like 'king' alongside feminine pronouns, resulting in phrases that seem almost poetic now. 'His Majesty, Herself' would make a wonderful social media bio, no?

Hatshepsut has been claimed as a feminist who defied gender rules to stick it to the patriarchy, as well as the world's first

transgender icon. Of course, none of these claims can be verified, and our insistence on defining the pharaoh's gender identity says more about our obsession with binary gender than it does about Hatshepsut. There have been centuries of debate as to *why* Hatshepsut expressed her gender in such a way, but all that debate misses the point: there doesn't need to be a reason.

Long live Her Majesty the King.

Far west of Cairo, across the Great Sand Sea of the Sahara Desert and towards the border of modern-day Libya, lies the Siwa Oasis. Surrounded by desert and dunes, the Siwa Oasis is a fertile pocket, home to sprawling date palms, olive trees and salt lakes, and has sustained a human settlement for more than twelve thousand years. It's not a place routinely accessed by outsiders, and today the community is primarily made up of Imazighen, or Berber people. It has, for its size, attracted a disproportionate amount of interest from anthropologists and archaeologists due to a feature of its historical civilisation: men having sex with each other.

Not only did Ancient Siwi men frequently and openly have sex with other men and boys, these relationships seem to have been formalised in unions similar to marriage. This custom appears to have survived through the Siwi's first contact with Pharaonic Egypt and then later the arrival of Islam, but over the last century the Egyptian government has sought to repress and erase it from history.

Although there are rumours of accepted, if not celebrated, same-sex relationships and diverse genders among ancient civilisations across the entire African continent, historians' efforts have focussed disproportionately on Ancient Egypt. Western historians often examine Egypt as part of the Levant (the Eastern Mediterranean area of West Asia, roughly made up of modern-day Lebanon, Syria, Iraq, Palestine, Israel and Jordan). This region has regularly been credited – wrongly – as the birthplace of civilisation, when in fact civilisation was developing in other parts of the world, such as China and India, at the same time. The Levant is, however, known for birthing two of the world's largest religions, which explains why it gets so much attention.

Within the Levant stood Mesopotamia (modern-day Iraq) and its capital, the ancient city of Babylon. Citizens of Babylon were very sex positive – anal sex was a common practice to avoid pregnancy and the Babylonians were big advocates of masturbation. To Babylonians, same-sex love and desire was generally a non-issue.

Things apparently changed when a man named Abram (later Abraham), who lived in Southern Mesopotamia, was sent by god to found a new nation. His journey of bringing a single god to the people of the Levant is documented in a series of ancient scriptures known as the Old Testament, or the Torah, or the Quran. Maybe you've heard of them?

If you weren't raised according to an Abrahamic religion, this bit might be hard to wrap your head around, as these scriptures are both religious texts and historical documents. There's evidence that some of the people and places described in these scriptures existed, though other accounts seem far less likely. But let's not get caught up in the debate over fact vs fiction because, regardless, the stories in these scriptures will fundamentally shape the course of LGBTQ+ history.

THE STORY OF
Sodomy

Heads up: the word 'sodomy' will appear a lot in this book. Bummer. Primarily it refers to anal sex between men, but throughout history it has also been used to refer to acts considered 'against god', like bestiality, or any sexual act that's not for procreation.

The story behind the word dates back to a biblical scripture called the Book of Genesis, written around 600 BCE. It contains the tale of two ancient cities known as Sodom and Gomorrah. These cities had angered god with their wickedness and sin, so god supposedly sent two angels to destroy them. Abraham – in the midst of his new nation project – had a nephew who lived in Sodom so asked god to spare the cities. God agreed, but only if fifty righteous people could be found there.

When the angels arrived, Abraham's nephew Lot welcomed them into the home he shared with his wife and children. Unfortunately, the men of Sodom got word of the visitors and demanded to 'know' them (in the biblical sense, this meant to have sex with them). Lot tried to bargain with them, offering his wife and virgin daughters up instead, but the angry men were determined to have their way with the angels.

Obviously there is nothing righteous about any of this, so a furious god rained fire and sulphur onto the towns of Sodom and Gomorrah, destroying them completely.

According to the dominant interpretation, the 'sin of Sodom' isn't the Sodomites' actions, which were very clearly rape – it is the fact that the angels were *male*.

If you're aghast at what is possibly history's worst ever case of victim-blaming, you're not alone. Many scholars share your thoughts, and some suggest it is more likely to have been the town's lack of hospitality that angered god. We don't actually know if these towns even existed, but we do know that this tale gave us the word 'sodomy' – and the enduring misconception that it's a sin.

Not long after the Book of Genesis was written, the Book of Leviticus came along. It's worth mentioning that these books were created over a long period of time – hundreds of years – and by multiple authors. Things change a lot over whole centuries, so these books should be thought of as an ever-evolving version of events, rather than some kind of group assignment. Different authors would make changes to existing phrasing – and frankly, the way passages have been edited reveals as much about the ideologies of the time as the details in the passages themselves.

The Book of Leviticus holds the most widely quoted (alleged) condemnation of homosexuality, but just like with the story of Sodom, this phrase might not be what it seems. The book says, 'You shall not lie with a male as with a woman; it is an abomination,' which okay, yes, seems fairly damning. But as always, context is key: this appears alongside many other confusing regulations about who you can or can't have sex with, including various family members and menstruating women. Scholars have said that the passage is actually condemning different forms of incest, and translators have argued that the original Hebrew shows it was only intended for some men, in some situations.

Either way, there are numerous rules in the Old Testament that modern religion says shouldn't be taken literally (ever heard the rule against wearing wool and linen at the same time?), yet for some reason the ones condemning homosexuality have been taken as doctrine. The impact of this will rear its head down the track, but for now, let's flag this as an isolated ideology in a rapidly changing world – and check in on the Greeks.

When we talk about Ancient Greece, we're talking less about a place and more about a people: the ethnic group known as the Greeks, or Hellenes. 'Ancient Greece' wasn't a country but a sprawling civilisation made up of many city-states (some historians say over one thousand) that were each ruled in accordance with different laws and cultures. Some were very influential – not just in ancient times, but in modern times too. If you've ever voted, you're harking back to Athens. If you've ever been to a Broadway show, you can thank Thebes. Olympia? You get the idea.

With so much modern Western culture stemming from Ancient Greek societies, it's no surprise how much queer culture we've gleaned from them too – including history's original lesbian.

KNOW YOUR ICONS
Sappho

The word 'lesbian' really just means 'person from Lesbos', an island just off the coast of Turkey. And on the island of Lesbos, right at the edge of Ancient Greece, lived a poet named Sappho.

Most historians place Sappho's birth somewhere between 640 and 610 BCE. Sappho was a very prolific poet, admired by many in her time, but only fragments of her work remain. Sappho wrote playfully and exquisitely about love and desire between women – hence the use of the words 'lesbian' and 'sapphic' to describe women who experience queer attraction. Despite being written thousands of years ago, the dramatic feelings Sappho describes in her poetry echo our experiences of love today. These next lines could easily be found in the messaging app of any modern lesbian.

I have had not one word from her
Frankly I wish I were dead
When she left, she wept
A great deal; she said to
Me, 'This parting must be
Endured, Sappho. I go unwillingly.'

We still can't really say that Sappho herself was a lesbian in the modern sense. All we know about her life is what her poetry indicates, and poetry isn't necessarily non-fiction.

It's probably worth stating the fairly obvious but still mind-bending fact that the Ancient Greeks lived a really long time ago. So long ago that there were historians of Ancient Greece *who lived in Ancient Greece*. The popular culture idea of Ancient Greece, with its sun-bleached stone pillars and wandering philosophers, is actually just one particular time period, known as the Classical Age. Sappho lived close to a century before this, in a period called the Archaic Era.

Greeks during the Classical Age were enamoured with Sappho. They wrote plays about her and documented her, but they were as close to sitting down and getting to know her as today's historians are to hanging out with Thomas Edison. They projected their Classical Era biases onto her, devaluing her work because she was female, sexualising her and perhaps even deliberately distorting her. This all helps explain why so much literature surrounding Sappho is relegated to interpretation.

In the many centuries since Sappho wrote of women wearing garlands of violets, every discovery made about her has thrown up more questions. Historians agree that her poetry would have been sung and accompanied by a lyre (a u-shaped stringed instrument). Beyond that, however, there are controversies surrounding almost every aspect of her life, including whether her work was ever performed in public and whether she had a daughter. But there is nothing more hotly debated than Sappho's sexuality. It's been suggested that she was a teacher or leader trusted with educating a collective of young women, and that Sappho's desire for these students was expressed in her poetry.

The truth is, we'll never know the truth. Arguing about the sexuality of a person who existed so long ago is pretty redundant, but for better or worse, Sappho has become a symbol. And it's easy to believe poetry that so viscerally describes desire between women could only have been written by a woman who'd felt it herself.

THE CASE OF
Lesbians Against Lesbians

Even though the word 'lesbian' originally means 'person from Lesbos', today the term definitely conjures up images of queer women, and people haven't always been happy about that.

In 2008, a group of Lesbians – as in, actual residents of Lesbos – felt their identity was being insulted through its association with gay women. They took the matter to a Greek court, asking it to ban the use of the term 'lesbian' to describe anything other than the island's population.

It was a tough and rather linguistically confusing court battle, with a lot of lesbians on both sides. To break it down, let's call the residents of Lesbos 'the plaintiffs' and the LGBTQ+ community and their allies 'the defendants'.

The plaintiffs argued that the island residents were the only true lesbians and, while conceding that gay women could define themselves as they wished, stated that they should not be able to appropriate the identity of people from Lesbos. The defendants, on the other hand, argued that the case itself was prejudiced, and that not all residents of the island were unhappy about the association. The term had also given the island a big tourism boost – Lesbos hosts a number of festivals for the LGBTQ+ community, and many queer folk see the trek to Sappho's birthplace as something of a pilgrimage.

Ultimately, the plaintiffs' attempt failed. The court decided that a single word did not define the identity of those from Lesbos, and ruled in favour of the defendants.

So now the word 'lesbian' can be used to describe a person from Lesbos, a woman who loves women, or – in the case of gay women who are from Lesbos – both.

The legend of Sappho isn't the only window we have into the changing values of Greek societies. Another poet of the Archaic Era who had an extraordinary impact on the later Greeks was Homer, the assumed author of *The Iliad*, an epic twenty-four book poem telling the story of the Trojan War. The text is placed around the eighth century BCE, but it is believed to have been a spoken poem that was passed down for centuries, until Homer finally wrote it down. Although historians generally agree that the Trojan War occurred, the characters are thought to be mythological, and the storyline is all legend.

The Iliad has everything – gods, heroes, that famous Trojan horse, and one of the most famous homoromantic love stories of all time.

THE GIST OF
Achilles and Patroclus

If you have a decent amount of time to fill, it's absolutely worth losing yourself in the real thing, but if you don't, here's a highly abridged version of *The Iliad* (or at least the parts relevant to this book). The hero of the story is Achilles, the greatest warrior in the world and the leader of the Greeks, who have been at war with the city of Troy for a decade. Achilles has a huge argument with the general of the Greek army and refuses to fight in the war anymore. He even asks his mother to pray to Zeus to help the Trojans. Who knew heroes could be this petty?

Enter Patroclus, Achilles' closest and most intimate companion. With Greece on the brink of losing the war against the Trojans, Patroclus tries to convince Achilles to re-join the fight, but alas, Achilles is having none of it. So Patroclus (the real hero here) goes to fight in the war himself, wearing the armour of his beloved companion.

Things are looking better for the Greeks, until Hector – Achilles' Trojan counterpart – kills Patroclus, mistaking him for Achilles. When Achilles finds out, he is devastated and furious. He returns to the war to avenge Patroclus, and after a long battle between the two warriors, Achilles kills Hector in the name of his beloved.

But Achilles didn't have to live without Patroclus for long, because the god Apollo knew about Achilles' one weakness – his heel, of course. Apollo guides a Trojan arrow into Achilles' heel, killing him. This is not the end of *The Iliad* (we haven't even reached the part about the Trojan horse!), but it is the tragic end of Achilles and Patroclus.

This kylix – an Ancient Greek wine-drinking cup – shows the fiery Achilles in a moment of tenderness toward a wounded Patroclus.

For millennia people have been fascinated by the story of Achilles (we even named a tendon after him), but the nature of his love for Patroclus has remained a source of debate. Some three hundred years later, in the Classical Era, Achilles and Patroclus were consistently depicted in art and theatre as lovers. Many artefacts show the usually arrogant Achilles being tender and kind to Patroclus. Upon Patroclus' death, Achilles is depicted naked, lying across his friend's chest, overcome with grief. The writer Aeschylus, known for his contribution to the Greek tragedies, wrote Achilles and Patroclus as tragic lovers, not too dissimilar to the way Shakespeare would describe them two thousand years later in *Troilus and Cressida*. Another four hundred years pass and Madeline Miller would write *The Song of Achilles*, in another one of the countless iterations of this timeless tale that explicitly place Achilles and Patroclus in a same-sex relationship.

We're not here to debate their sexuality, and there is no progress to be made by suggesting that two men having a close and loving friendship is proof they are 'gay'. What can be debated, however, is how Homer intended to write them and what interpretations of their story can tell us about queer love in Ancient Greece.

One other highly influential Ancient World figure who argued that Patroclus and Achilles were in a same-sex relationship was the philosopher Plato in his monumental work *The Symposium*. This text has been a source of validation to same-sex attracted and asexual people for thousands of years.

In *The Symposium*, Plato tells the story of a group of philosophers, comedians and writers who come together to drink and talk. If you've ever compiled the guest list for your dream dinner party, you're essentially creating your own version of Plato's Symposium. It unfolds like a sort of drunken public-speaking competition, where each guest stands up to deliver a speech on the nature of romantic love and desire, or *eros* as it was called then.

During the evening's final speech, Plato's teacher Socrates describes a 'ladder of love', beginning with physical love and ascending towards intellectual and ethereal love, which were considered 'higher forms'. This higher love was given the name 'Platonic', after Plato. Today this term is generally understood to mean love that is not sexual, and is perhaps regarded as a lesser form of love. But according to the forefather of Western philosophy, it's the opposite. This definition can be very affirming for people on the asexual spectrum, as it shows us that sex is not a pre-requisite for worthy, deep and valid relationships.

Other men at the Symposium went even further with their praise of same-sex love. It was here that Phaedrus came up with the idea for an army made up entirely of male lovers, suggesting that such an army could defeat the entire world. According to Phaedrus, 'The veriest coward would become an inspired hero, equal to the bravest, at such a time; Love would inspire him.'

This fresco shows a scene from *The Symposium,* and you don't need a fine art degree to decipher the homoeroticism within it.

Ancient Greece's Queer Answer to Adam and Eve

Another highlight of *The Symposium* is comic playwright Aristophanes telling a queer creation story that explains why people feel whole when they find love.

According to Aristophanes, humans were once doubles – beings with four feet, four hands and two sets of genitals – and there were not two sexes, but three: one sex comprising of man and man, one of woman and woman, and a third of man and woman, known as androgynous. The men were born from the sun, women from the Earth, and androgynous from the moon.

When the humans angered Zeus, he severed them in two, leaving them to go through life seeking their other halves. Men and women from the androgynous would find each other and be able to mate. Women from the original woman would not desire men, and instead become each other's partners, while men from the original man would continue life together in sexual satisfaction.

It may sound absurd, but no more so than the story of Adam and Eve and their forbidden fruit.

Aristophanes does say that the ideal form of love is a relationship between men, because this is the most manly – which makes sense if you equate manliness with goodness like the Greeks did. But what is remarkable in this story is that these attractions are presented as three equally viable combinations – and that tells us a lot about attitudes to same-sex relationships at this time.

The Symposium would make an excellent basis for a reality television show – there was plenty of drama among the drinking and philosophy. Some of the speeches had the secondary agenda of getting another guest into bed, and at one point someone drunkenly crashes the party to lament that Socrates won't sleep with him. There was even one committed same-sex couple there: Agathon and Pausanias. In his speech, Pausanias argued in favour of same-sex eros, in particular the virtue of the love between an older man and a boy around the age when he begins to grow a beard.

Relationships between men and boys are a well-documented phenomenon of Ancient Greece. The practice, known as pederasty, involved the pairing of an erastes (an older, more experienced man) with an eromenos (a more youthful boy). It was considered a mutually beneficial trade – the younger received tutelage and guidance, while the older received sexual satisfaction. It seems that in some societies, such as Athens, pederastic relationships were primarily confined to the elite social classes, while in Spartan society they were more of a rite of passage, a mandatory part of the progression into adulthood.

The age gap appeared to vary according to the unique culture and customs of the different city-states. The eromenos would be an adolescent boy anywhere between the ages of twelve and eighteen, while the erastes was a man who had reached adulthood but was not *old*. Typically, they would be in their twenties.

There were many rules: the erastes could be punished if he were deemed to be too keenly pursuing a younger boy, while the eromenos had to be careful not to seduce an older man, or he could face penalties for prostitution. It was important that the eromenos was not seen to be forced into the relationship, even though it couldn't exactly be considered free will.

The roles within the relationships were also strictly laid out. The word 'erastes' roughly translates to lover, while the word 'eromenos' means beloved. The distinction between who was doing the loving and who was being loved was fundamentally important – the older man must be the active participant, while the younger must take the passive role. However, if the younger man continued to take the passive role once he came of age, he would be mocked.

There are many (usually quite explicit) artworks of the period depicting these relationships. These can be very confronting, especially when we view them through the lens of our modern ethics, which would categorically say that such a power dynamic would mean consent is impossible. However, even if these relationships would be unethical – and in most places illegal – today, it is vital to understand that pederasty is not paedophilia. This is a challenging part of queer history to navigate, as the conflation of homosexuality with paedophilia continues to harm our community, even today.

THE PASSION OF
The Cut Sleeve

The Ancient Greeks have a reputation for same-sex liaisons, but all the way over in Ancient China, they were just as popular. You've probably experienced the agony of observing your partner (or pet, for that matter) sleeping sweetly beside you, their precious head on your arm. That closeness is lovely – until you realise you need to pee. This same thing happened to Emperor Ai of Han Dynasty China (206 BCE – 220 CE).

It's said that Emperor Ai and his lover Dong Xian were enjoying a nap together at the Palace in Chang'an (which is now Xi'an in China). When the emperor awoke, he found Dong Xian lying asleep on the sleeve of his robe. Rather than risk waking his beloved, he simply cut off his sleeve. Word of this tender act spread throughout the palace, and soon Emperor Ai's courtiers began cutting off their own sleeves as a tribute to the emperor's show of affection. The single-sleeve robe became something of a trend, and a euphemism for same-sex love was born. Even today in China, same-sex love is referred to as 'the passion of the cut sleeve'.

Emperor Ai certainly wasn't the only Han Dynasty emperor to have a male lover – all ten emperors were said to have had relationships with other men alongside their wives. The idea of having male and female partners was normalised in China during this period. Sima Qian, a Chinese historian of the early Han Dynasty (who himself lived before Emperor Ai, but documented the phenomenon of these male 'favourites'), wrote 'It is not women alone who can use their looks to attract the eyes of the ruler; courtiers and eunuchs can play that game as well. Many were the men of ancient times who gained favour this way.'

The emperor's male lovers received exceedingly special treatment, which was entirely accepted – so long as the emperor produced an heir with his empress. But Emperor Ai did not produce an heir. No surviving records show that Emperor Ai was ever interested in women, and the favouritism shown towards Dong Xian soon became an issue in the palace. Not only was the emperor rewarding Dong Xian with grain, he also bestowed great gifts and important titles upon his family.

As Emperor Ai's health declined with illness, Dong Xian's power at the palace rose dramatically, until the emperor, on his death bed, expressed his desire to leave the entire kingdom to Dong Xian. This, unfortunately, was too much for the court, who stepped in and forced Dong Xian and his wife to kill themselves.

There are other tales of same-sex desire from Ancient China, and they all have this almost parabolic quality to them. Historian Bret Hinsch in his book *Passions of the Cut Sleeve* notes that the way narrative and meaning have been written around these events shows a consciousness around same-sex love that has helped subsequent generations of queer people see themselves in history. This story shows us that over two thousand years ago, people in China were moved by same-sex love, just as they are today, and that the desire to let sleeping lovers lie is part of us, wherever and whenever we are.

The practice we now refer to as 'bottom shaming' – something that the queer and trans community is still struggling to shake – is an ancient problem. Masculinity was highly valued in ancient societies, and taking the 'woman's role' was considered weak. (The obvious question, of course, is how there can be any top without a bottom.) This would be mitigated by ensuring that your 'bottom' was of a lesser social standing than you. In this sense, it's very difficult to separate sex in ancient societies from power and class.

In Greek societies this nuanced distinction between sex and class was grounded in ideas of virtue, but when the Romans conquered the Greeks in the first century BCE, they took their top/bottom politics to a whole new level. Ancient history tends to be chapterised according to its conquests, and in Roman society sex was viewed in the same way – the top being the conqueror, the bottom, the conquered. 'Conquering' someone was considered a masculine act, so sex between men was entirely accepted – so long as you were the top. Roman dictator Julius Caesar was known for his sexual escapades with both women and men, but was frequently mocked for being on the receiving end.

We also know that sex between men in Ancient Rome was wildly common, because the Romans didn't write about these explicit acts in secret – they put them all over the city's walls. When Mount Vesuvius erupted, covering the ancient city of Pompeii in ash and perfectly preserving it, we weren't just given a snapshot of life at the time, but a range of pornographic material proving that sex between men frequently occurred for pleasure, and that there were many bottoms that relished in their role.

As is unfortunately the case in many times and places, rape and sexual assault was used in Ancient Rome as a way to affirm masculinity, assert control or shame a person, but there were also many instances of sex between two men who both had agency and were willing participants. To make this distinction, historians have looked to language. The Romans had different words (rude ones) for the same sexual act that indicated whether it was willing or forced. Similarly, verbs in Latin have active and passive constructions that help linguists and historians pinpoint who had agency in different situations.

Basically, grammar is very important.

Antinous and Hadrian

Sex in Ancient Rome wasn't always without love. Emperor Hadrian, who ruled the Roman Empire from 117 to 138 CE, became so intoxicated by a boy named Antinous, he had him turned into a god.

Hadrian was said to be unhappily married and disinterested in other women, but when he met the Bithynian peasant boy Antinous he immediately fell in love. Antinous had the kind of angelic beauty that would capture the sensibilities of writers and artists for centuries, but Hadrian believed him wise and intelligent as well. Their relationship was pederastic; Antinous was just thirteen when Hadrian took him as his lover. Antinous accompanied Hadrian on his travels, making their way from Athens to Alexandria.

Just before Antinous' twentieth birthday, as he and Hadrian were sailing down the Nile, Antinous fell overboard and drowned. How this happened remains a mystery – and a suspicious one at that. There is no documentation from the time that describes the death of Antinous as an accident; speculation covers off everything from murder to suicide and sacrifice.

Hadrian was so devastated by the death of his beloved that he had him deified. Emperors could become gods, but it was highly unusual for a boy of unremarkable origins like Antinous to be given this status. Hadrian went further and announced that a city would be built in his honour, named Antinoöpolis. He also founded a cult to be devoted to Antinous, which was followed by people all across the empire.

The cult of Antinous dissolved as Christianity became dominant, but in later centuries he continued to be unofficially worshipped in art and literature – especially by those who were same-sex attracted.

At this point in our timeline, we've crossed over the threshold of the Common Era, which in the Christian tradition refers to the birth of Jesus.

While today Jesus is one of the most well-documented figures of all time – and most scholars agree that such a person did exist – when he did walk the Earth, he was nowhere near as famous. For the next few centuries under the Roman Empire, most Romans were Jewish or polytheist, meaning they worshipped multiple deities as opposed to one god. Later, the Catholic Church would refer to these people as pagans.

One of the most well-known pagan emperors also happens to be one of the oldest figures on record who we could reasonably say might have been transgender.

Elagabalus

Emperor Elagabalus, sometimes called Heliogabalus, was born in modern-day Syria under the Roman Empire. She was assigned male at birth and given the name Antoninus. Before ascending to the throne of the Roman Empire, she was a high priestess of the pagan sun god Elagabal, hence the name Elagabalus. She only lived for eighteen years and reigned for just four, but in her short life she was notorious.

Elagabalus defied all masculine conventions of the time, and her contemporaries wrote of her wearing make-up and wigs. Roman historian Cassius Dio describes Elagabalus announcing, 'Call me not lord, for I am a lady,' as well as offering vast sums to any physician who could provide her with a vagina. She married four women but only had eyes for the young enslaved chariot-racer Hierocles, and delighted in calling herself his mistress, wife and queen.

She was cruel and extravagant, keeping lions and tigers as pets and sending them out after dessert to terrify dinner guests. A nineteenth-century painting titled *The Roses of Heliogabalus* depicts a moment she allegedly rained flowers onto her guests, suffocating and crushing them to death.

Elagabalus' extravagance and blatant disregard for the rules of gender angered the Roman Army and Senate, so in 222 CE she was assassinated, and her body thrown in the river Tiber. After her death, the Roman Senate issued something called a *Damnatio memoriae*, or a condemnation of memory, which mandated Elagabalus to be excluded from all records. Despite the best efforts of the Roman establishment, Elagabalus wasn't erased; in fact, she has become renowned as the transgender icon of Ancient Rome.

Back in the third century CE when Elagabalus reigned, Christianity was still emerging. Early Christians were heavily persecuted under the Roman Empire for their one-godded ways.

However, things would change at the beginning of the next century, when Emperor Constantine allegedly saw a cross in the sky before the Battle of the Milvian Bridge in 312 CE. Constantine claimed this vision was a divine symbol that helped his army win the battle, and so became the first Roman emperor to convert to Christianity. Some historians argue that Constantine's conversion was for political reasons, and his vision merely a convenient cover story, but either way, this moment was a turning point for the church – and kicked off centuries of suffering for LGBTQ+ people.

We will move through this bit fairly swiftly, but it's still a lot to take in, so you might want to brace yourself.

When Constantine converted, he legalised the practice of Christianity and supported its spread. By the time Emperor Theodosius I began his reign in 379 CE, the Roman Catholic Church was so established that the emperor made it the only recognised religion under the Roman Empire. Now, under the steadfastly Christian Theodosius, it was the pagans and Jews who fled persecution. As part of his crusade, Theodosius would develop a Code, which historians believe was a kind of wish list of laws that would govern his ideal Catholic state. One of these laws decreed that men should not 'marry in the manner of a woman'. This had nothing to do with interpretation of the Christian scriptures and more to do with stamping out practices associated with paganism.

It was in 534 CE, under the Byzantine Empire (also known as the Eastern Roman Empire), that Emperor Justinian I used Christian scripture to justify the prohibition of sexuality. The world was going through a period of environmental instability at the time, and a series of earthquakes, famines and plagues had people spooked. To maintain control, Justinian needed a scapegoat. Remember the story of Sodom and Gomorrah? Using an interpretation of this story, Justinian decreed that just as god had destroyed the town of Sodom, so too had he sent these natural disasters as punishment for same-sex relations – therefore, to stop the disasters, this behaviour would be decreed a sin, punishable by death. Nice.

Using homosexuality as a scapegoat for environmental bad luck really caught on; homosexuality would be blamed for all manner of disasters over the next few thousand years.

The fall of the Western Roman Empire in 476 CE is generally considered to be the end of Classical Antiquity. We began this chapter in a world of many beliefs and many gods. New ideas proliferated and sophisticated societal structures formed. Relationships were about wealth and politics, while sex was a pleasure to be enjoyed, regardless of where it was found. It seems like a series of unhappy accidents that led to the point where same-sex relations were blamed for natural disasters, declared a sin and punished by death.

The persecution of same-sex relations had nothing to do with morality, ethics or faith, and everything to do with power. And that power was about to really take hold, in the form of organised religion.

CHAPTER TWO

The Queer Ecstatic

The collapse of the Western Roman Empire ushered in the Middle Ages, a messy period of history marked by a restructure of society. The Byzantine Empire continued to hold across Eastern and Southern Europe, while Germanic peoples set up kingdoms in the former Roman Empire. Soaring high above all this was the Catholic Church, controlled by the emperor in the East and the pope in the West.

Eventually, the Catholic Church would split away from the Byzantine Church (which would become the Eastern Orthodox Church) over a disagreement about unleavened bread, but for now the most important thing to stress is just how powerful the church had become.

The Catholic Church had tremendous influence over every echelon of society, from peasants to the king, but during the early Middle Ages, it wasn't too concerned with same-sex acts – after all, the portion of the scriptures that mentioned this was extremely minor in comparison to everything else they contained. Even if the church condemned same-sex liaisons on the basis of Sodom and Gomorrah, this was rarely enforced. There are even instances of bishops and other respected clergy members having male lovers and facing no punishment (let's be frank, corruption has been a part of the church since its inception). Primarily, the Catholic Church was motivated by expanding its power.

By the twelfth century, however, the church deemed any sexual activity not for the purpose of procreation a sin. The sin of sodomy didn't just include same-sex relations – it also extended to masturbation, oral sex, anal sex, and sex with animals.

Of course, it was difficult to prove these acts had occurred, so most people who faced trial for sodomy were unlikely to have actually committed the 'sin' in question – at least, not when they were accused of having done so. Mostly, sodomy was a useful hook to hang your enemies on.

THE ORDER OF
Catholic Warrior Monks Who Were Burnt for Kissing Each Other's Butts

The Knights Templar was a military order of the Catholic Church that was founded during the Crusades. The order was made up of devout Catholic warrior monks who gave protection to pilgrims visiting the Holy Land of Jerusalem. The Templar also established an early form of banking across the Christian Empire. They were extremely wealthy, and lent a lot of money to King Phillip IV of France.

The king's debt to the Templar grew, and he needed a way out. Luckily for him, there had been rumours of secret initiation rites among the Templar that involved 'kissing' senior members in obscene places (including but not limited to the mouth, buttocks, anus, and lower back) as well practising witchcraft. The king, an opportunistic fellow, used the rumours to his advantage, announcing an inquisition into this rumoured butt-kissing.

Under interrogation by order of the king, the Knights Templar confessed to obscene sexual practices, including the aforementioned kissing, as well as heresy and worshipping a horned deity with three faces. These 'confessions', however, can't be taken at face value because 'interrogation' meant torture – the knights would have admitted to almost anything. Most of the Templars eventually retracted their confessions, but this wasn't much help. Many were burned at the stake for their transgressions, and the king forced the pope to disband the order.

The tale of the Templar has long been a source of intrigue. The horned deity the monks allegedly worshipped has become a prominent occult symbol associated with modern mysticism, while an oft-told legend that the Templar were the keepers of the Holy Grail was given new life in the 2000s thanks to Dan Brown's best-selling novel *The Da Vinci Code*.

It's impossible to know if there's truth to any of these rumours, but you know what they say: where there's smoke, there's fire. It is highly likely that homosexuality was practised among the Templar as well as in other monastic orders. Monks were sworn to celibacy (with women), and travelled vast distances with only themselves for company. It's likely there were certain initiation rites with a sexual element to them – after all, sex has been used to these ends throughout history all over the world. Written artefacts of the time show that these monastic orders didn't view same-sex practices with any particular disdain, which speaks volumes, as monks lived very rule-oriented lives. And hey, if you were a man who happened to be same-sex attracted, what could be better than being forced to swear off female flesh and ride out your days in the company of men?

The Medieval period in Western Europe is often painted by historians as a rather uncivilised time, characterised by little scientific progress and a lot of burning at the stake. This might be a rather biased summary of events, as we'll explore a little later. But if we travel further east through the Byzantine Empire into the region that expands from modern-day Egypt in North Africa all the way to Pakistan in Western Asia, we will arrive in the dynasty known as the Abbasid Caliphate, which ruled the region from 750 to 1258 CE. By contrast to the Western medieval world, which was a tad chaotic after the fall of Rome, this period under the Abbasid Caliphate was not only stable, but known for its intellectual, scientific and cultural development, emanating from the caliphate's centre in Baghdad. For this reason, life under the Abbasid Caliphate is known as the Islamic Golden Age.

During this period, Islamic scholars translated a whole lot of Ancient Greek texts and circulated them through madaris networks (the schools and universities of the time). Plato's ideas about intellectual and spiritual love between men being more sustainable and closer to the divine than physical love began to influence society. Here, just like in Ancient Greece, young boys were idolised as objects of beauty – so much so that Sufi scholars advised against looking at them to reduce the risk of falling in love.

In poetry, young men are described as having cheeks of rose and lips of sugar. Pages are full of rapturous blazing romances between men, longing embraces – even kisses. But was it sexual? We need a little more context.

In medieval Islamic society beauty was considered masculine rather than feminine, which is perhaps because women were kept completely hidden. Men didn't encounter women until marriage, so during their youth they would form deep emotional and romantic bonds with each other. Young men were desired by older men in the same way they were in Ancient Greece and elsewhere at different points in history. But there's an important distinction. Lustful sex between men was condemned, and those who committed it were considered the People of Lot. (Remember, the story of Sodom and Gomorrah exists in the Bible, the Quran *and* the Torah.)

It's interesting to pause and reflect on what we consider 'sexual' and where we get those ideas from. Acts like kissing are so often framed in the West as the gateway to getting it on, but these distinctions feel pretty arbitrary when you think about it. By the same token, it doesn't make sense to say that these loving romances between men weren't queer. Far too often queer love is viewed as purely sexual, and while it absolutely can be sexual, it can be every bit as deep and spiritual as the love described in these mystic poems.

So when referring to the love and sexuality in the Golden Age of Islam, we don't need to go so far as to call it homosexual; instead, a better word might be 'homosensual'. And there's one poet who can teach us all about that.

KNOW YOUR ICONS
Rumi

Jalāl al-Dīn Rumi was born in Persia in 1207 and was raised
according to Sufism, a brand of Islamic mysticism concerned with
awakening a Muslim's spirituality through direct experiences with
god. Rumi found this direct connection through poetry, which he
was believed to recite while whirling around and around in a state of
religious rhapsody. This practice gave rise to a group of followers
known as the whirling dervishes, who continued this style of moving
meditation in Rumi's name after his death.

Rumi never wrote a word down; however, he had a circle of
dedicated scribes who compiled collections of his work. Rumi's
poetry burns with divine love and has captivated much of the world's
imagination for centuries.

A major revival in the mid 2000s led to Rumi being crowned the
highest-selling poet in the United States.

Rumi's wisdom on love famously helped Coldplay's Chris Martin navigate his divorce from Gwyneth Paltrow, and his phrasings have been stylised on JPEGs of long-exposure night skies and shared all over the internet tagged #inspo and #foodforthought. You'll find Rumi's work on Ivanka Trump's Twitter and even tattooed just near Brad Pitt's right armpit. Sadly, Rumi's most well-known words have been lost in translation – we'd recommend doing your due diligence before immortalising them on your skin or wedding invitations.

Another thing that has been lost in the mythologisation of Rumi is that he was first and foremost a Muslim.

Rumi, like his father, was a Sufi scholar. He rose to become an eminent teacher in Islamic law and circulated among the highest echelons of Islamic society. Alongside his mysticism and poetry, he practised Islam throughout his life, praying and fasting and offering his interpretations of Islamic law. But when Rumi met Shams Tabrizi in 1244 CE, everything changed.

Shams became Rumi's beloved teacher, soulmate and new subject of Rumi's poetry. The two were inseparable. Rumi wrote of Shams like one might write of a god; in fact, the distinction between the two isn't exactly clear. His writing became increasingly homoerotic, including phrases like:

I am your harp,
You strike me like a plectrum
On every part of my body
How can't I cry?

Rumi and Shams locked themselves away for forty nights to speak and exchange ideas about divine love, and it's been suggested that here their love took on a physical element.

Rumi and Shams were together for a short time – only two years – before Shams mysteriously disappeared. He may have been killed out of jealousy by someone close to Rumi, or he may have simply left. All we know is that Rumi was left consumed by grief.

Whether their relationship was physical or platonic, its queerness is in the pain of separation. In finding love and losing it, countless queer people have felt that white-hot pain.

When the Abbasid Caliphate fell to the Mongol Empire in the mid thirteenth century, the instability and destruction brought the Golden Age of Islam to an end. But further west in Italy, a new 'Golden Age' was just getting started. An influx of Jewish and Muslim scholars from the East brought with them the same Ancient Greek texts that had been studied in the Abbasid Caliphate, which were then translated into Latin and rediscovered by the West. This was the dawn of the Renaissance, a highly romanticised period of history that closed the book on the Middle Ages. The word 'Renaissance' means 'rebirth', and refers to a renewed interest in Classical art, philosophy and culture, and that occurred throughout Europe from the mid thirteenth century right up until the seventeenth century.

Renaissance historians often talk about this period as a return to the sophistication of Ancient Greek and Latin culture, from the 'uncivilised' Middle Ages, when society mindlessly followed the Catholic Church without reason or critical thought. Many of these historians were *from* the Renaissance period, so there's definitely some bias at play here. There were many innovations birthed from the Renaissance, such as the Gutenberg printing press and single point perspective artwork, but it wasn't all golden-hued paintings and mathematical instruments. There were also a lot of people dying for their religious beliefs in violent wars across Europe.

Today we live in a constant cycle of throwbacks where what's old is considered new again so often that we barely notice, but the phenomenon of the Renaissance is not so different from our recurrent obsession with the 90s. The Classical period felt much more romantic and ethereal to thirteenth-century artists and philosophers, so they decided to bring it back.

This is why the Renaissance, particularly in Italy, was so undeniably queer. Men who slept with men were given the teachings of Plato as a way to justify the virtue in their desire. Renaissance thinkers built on the ideas presented in *The Symposium*, believing that intellectual love (between men, that is – women weren't thought to possess much of an intellect back then) brought one closer to god. Pederasty also made a comeback.

Sodomy was so prevalent in Renaissance Florence that the city had to do something, or at least *appear* to do something, to stop it – since technically it was still forbidden according to the church.

An administration called the Office of the Night was set up to tackle the issue. Most of those investigated for sodomy were fined and sent on their way, suggesting that the relationship between the Office of the Night and the city's sodomites was, to some extent, mutually beneficial. The fines, which were relatively minor, acted more like a tax, allowing the city to make considerable money off its citizens.

And remember Antinous, the angelic young lover of the Roman Emperor Hadrian who lived well over a thousand years ago? Like a fifteenth-century Timothée Chalamet, Antinous became the 'it boy' of the Renaissance. Artists of the era painted and sculpted young Antinous until he became the epitome of male beauty, and a regular face around the Louvre.

Speaking of which, the halls of the Louvre are littered with writhing, naked, muscular men who we can thank the Renaissance for. It's difficult to escape the homoerotic gaze of artists like Michelangelo and da Vinci, whose work is a window into the queer sensibilities of the time.

47

Leonardo da Vinci

Leonardo da Vinci is one of these unmistakably queer figures who were pivotal to the Renaissance. This polymath was born in Tuscany in 1452, the illegitimate son of a Florentine legal notary and an orphaned woman. Despite his unremarkable origins and struggles with writing (he was left-handed), Leonardo was excellent at just about everything.

Da Vinci started out as a studio assistant to painter and sculptor Andrea del Verrocchio, under whom other brilliant Renaissance artists like Botticelli also studied. In his late teens, Leonardo would become Verrocchio's apprentice and mastered not just painting and sculpting, but other technical skills like mechanics, which revolutionised his practice.

This is not Leonardo da Vinci but his very homoerotic oil painting of John the Baptist.

He became an expert on anatomy, working to understand the mechanics of the human body and re-create them accurately on the page. His *Vitruvian Man* sketch is a particularly famous example. Da Vinci blended art and mathematics to render realistic illustrations of his own inventions, including the helicopter and the parachute, which centuries later have come to fruition. These sketches have been repeatedly deemed the work of a true genius, yet none of them compare to his paintings, which are among the most famous artworks in the world. But there is one detail that is often overlooked: the model.

Leonardo painted one person more than any other, a young man named Gian Giacomo Caprotti, who da Vinci nicknamed Salaí, meaning 'little devil'. Salaí came to study under da Vinci when he was just ten years old, and was da Vinci's companion for years. Eventually, the two become lovers in what was presumably a pederastic relationship.

Da Vinci never seemed to tire of Salaí's angelic face and curls. His wildly homoerotic portrait of John the Baptist holding a suggestive finger in the air is widely believed to be based on Salaí. Slightly less unanimous is the suggestion that if you look at John the Apostle, to the left of Jesus in da Vinci's celebrated *Last Supper*, you'll see Salaí again.

Finally – and most controversially – Mona Lisa herself is said to be da Vinci's male lover.

This theory was spearheaded by Italian researcher and art detective Silvano Vinceti in 2016, after he used infrared technology to compare paintings of Salaí with the *Mona Lisa*. Vinceti noted striking similarities between the two faces, particularly around the nose, the forehead and that famous smile.

Leonardo da Vinci finished the *Mona Lisa* in France, and if you take the letters in M-O-N-A L-I-S-A and rearrange them, you get M-O-N S-A-L-A-I, meaning 'My Salaí' in French. Perhaps it is pure coincidence, or perhaps it was a code, a queer love letter to Salaí hidden in the most famous painting of all time.

Though concentrated in Italy, the Renaissance was a period of cultural reckoning across Europe when the dominant ideologies of the previous centuries were all up for debate. Not even the might of the Catholic Church could escape the scrutiny of the new intelligentsia.

Throughout the Middle Ages, the church had grown extremely wealthy off the people, and it showed in the gilded castles and decadent churches occupying prime real estate in every city. The cracks of corruption were beginning to show, and they caught the eye of a German man named Martin Luther.

Luther believed that instead of getting the word of god from the pope (who he suspected was more focussed on decadence and power than worship), people should actually pick up the Bible. Luther's back-to-basics approach to Christianity won him a dedicated following, and as a result the Catholic Church splintered and new branches of Christianity emerged. One was named after Luther himself – Lutheranism – and this, along with the other new branches, fell under what we know as Protestantism.

This new brand of Christianity centred around the scriptures and involved each person making a personal 'covenant' with god. The rise of Protestantism had the secondary effect of increasing literacy, because Protestants were actually required to read the Bible, whereas under the Catholic Church, you had the clergy to tell you what to do. This development, combined with the emergence of the printing press in Europe, meant many more people had access to the Bible and as a result, were introduced to our old friends the Book of Leviticus and Sodom and Gomorrah.

Historians tend to describe this period as the Reformation, as it marked a series of reforms to Christianity. The first Reformation, which swept across continental Europe, was soon followed by an English Reformation. This too was characterised by a shift towards Protestantism, but for a slightly different reason – the king of England, King Henry VIII, wanted a divorce. The Roman Catholic Church refused to allow this, so, in a fairly audacious power move, the king decided to make his own religion, which he was the head of: the Church of England. As you might have guessed, this new brand of Christianity was fine with divorce.

King Henry VIII decreed his new church the only official church of England. However, winding back centuries of Catholic influence was always going to be a big ask; he needed a way to wrench power from the Catholic Church.

During this period, some offences still came under the jurisdiction of the ecclesiastical courts, which reported into Rome. Sodomy, which in England was called buggery, was one such offence. In a breathtakingly petty move that would go on to cause centuries of pain, King Henry VIII made buggery a civil offence, signing into law the Buggery Act 1533. Now, for the first time, there was a civil law prohibiting sodomy. This would form the precedent for anti-homosexuality laws around the world.

In other words, King Henry VIII has a lot to answer for.

But the fun doesn't end there. Some people in England believed that the Church of England was stopping short of its Protestant potential, so a group of fundamentalist Protestants emerged. This group, known as the Puritans, made life very difficult for those who were same-sex attracted.

Puritans lived austere lives of restraint, eschewing all earthly pleasures in favour of worshipping and studying the Bible. They loathed all things frivolous, but none more than the theatre. Oh, and cross-dressing. They really hated that.

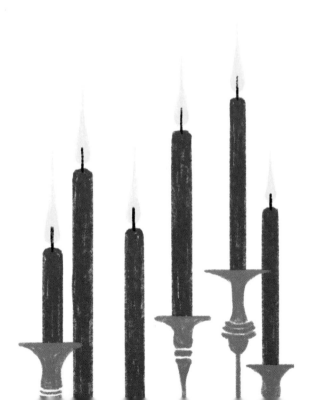

Shakespeare

William Shakespeare is widely regarded as the greatest writer of the English language, and his stories tap into the human condition so well they feel eternally relevant. As well as his mastery of words, Shakespeare's ideas of gender were way ahead of their time.

During this period, the theatre was a popular part of English life and a solid source of entertainment. Women, however, weren't allowed to perform on stage. They were required to remain pious at all times, and absolutely could not take part in such an ungodly spectacle. Women performing for an audience in exchange for money was associated with sex work, which was also considered extremely ungodly.

Shakespeare ostensibly navigated this by having boys play women's roles. It may have been better than women participating in these 'intolerable mischiefs to churches' (as Puritan William Prynne described it), but the Puritans were horrified by the idea of cross-dressing, especially if it continued off stage.

Although the Puritans held a lot of power, it appears that Shakespeare actually baited them in his plays. In *As You Like It*, Shakespeare weaves the act of cross-dressing into the story, writing a female character who dresses in men's clothing. Surely this boy dressing as a woman dressing as a man situation could only be some kind of Puritan dog whistle? In *Twelfth Night*, Shakespeare goes even further, including another deliberately cross-dressing character, but also a Puritan character, Malvolio, who is portrayed as hypocritical, selfish and power hungry.

It would have been highly risky for Shakespeare to invert gender roles in the way that he did, so we can only assume these choices were deliberate – perhaps an act of defiance and protest, or some kind of camp inside joke.

Shakespeare's own gender and sexuality are the subject of constant debate. He was married (to someone named Anne Hathaway, which has birthed a conspiracy theory that the modern actress Anne Hathaway's husband Adam Shulman is actually a reincarnation of Shakespeare – there's a striking resemblance between the two) and had children. However, at this time marriage, love and sex remained separate spheres. Many of his sonnets appear to be directed towards a young man and contain homoerotic wordplay. Of course, poetry isn't always autobiographical. But a good many Shakespeare scholars believe his sexuality aligned with what today we might call bisexual or queer. And let's face it, any enemy of the Puritans was probably a friend of ours.

With all sorts of lewd, ungodly spectacles cropping up, the Puritans began to feel the Church of England was beyond reform. Their initiatives to cleanse the people of sin and refocus them on the study of the Bible were proving futile. They needed a place where they could practise their branch of Protestantism freely and ban all the ghastly things that horrified them, such as long hair, slashed sleeves and lace with gold thread.

So when word spread of a new land – one not even mentioned in the Bible – the Puritans seized the opportunity to spread their faith with fervour. They soon found themselves on board a boat to New England, which would come to be known as America.

The only problem was, they had no business being there.

CHAPTER THREE

God, Gold and Glory

If there's one part of history that has caused more hurt to queer and transgender people than almost any other, it's colonisation. Of course, colonisation didn't only affect those who were same-sex attracted or gender diverse – it irreparably harmed countless Indigenous peoples across the world – however, its impact on LGBTQ+ people is too rarely spoken about.

The seventeenth century was part of what is often called the Age of Exploration, which sounds far more lofty and much less violent than the reality. During this period, European countries embarked on long voyages by sea to 'discover new lands' and establish colonies there. Their motivations are often summed up as 'god, gold and glory'. Let's unpack them.

First up is god. Now, European governments who wanted to establish colonies needed a lot of people to run them. That meant they had to convince people to board a dangerous boat and maybe get scurvy, so they tapped into one of history's greatest motivators: the word of god. Luckily, the sheer amount of people in the 1600s who were high on religion meant this wasn't a problem – and they genuinely believed they were doing god's work by introducing him to far-flung lands.

During the Age of Exploration, Christian missionaries of all denominations boarded boats bound for colonies in the Americas, Asia and the Pacific. Once they arrived, they were met by the Indigenous peoples of the lands they were intent on occupying, and set about building churches and converting these people to Christianity.

The missionaries felt they were helping Indigenous peoples, but in reality, they were doing the opposite. Colonial armies were inflicting mass murders, introducing disease and stealing land, so those Indigenous people who did convert to Christianity really didn't have a choice. Some of those who converted did so in the hope of retaining land rights, some were convinced this foreign god would ease their suffering, and some were forced through brutality.

As part of the process of colonisation, Indigenous peoples were forced to relinquish their own cultural practices and adopt European farming methods and Christian ideas of gender. But Indigenous peoples around the world have always had their own concepts of gender, which are overwhelmingly older and more diverse than those of the Christian Europeans.

In North America, rigid categories of gender didn't exist in most Indigenous cultures, which celebrated fluidity and even acknowledged multiple genders. In their eyes, cross-dressing was deeply spiritual and culturally sacred. Different words are used across different languages to describe people who embody both masculine and feminine energies in a way that is neither entirely male nor female. An umbrella term often used by these sacred peoples to describe themselves is 'two-spirit'.

We'wha

One of the most historically celebrated two-spirit people is a Zuni cultural leader known as We'wha.

We'wha was born in 1849 on the land now known by its colonial name of New Mexico. In Zuni culture, gender isn't assigned at birth, it's something acquired through life. By the time We'wha was four years old, it was obvious they were lhamana – the Zuni name for a person who is anatomically male, yet presents female. Lhamana were cultural leaders who possessed some skills attributed to men, but mostly trained in women's roles. We'wha was a highly skilled craftsperson who mastered both pottery and weaving. They were one of the first Zuni people to begin to sell their work, bringing visibility to Zuni arts.

The revered status of lhamana piqued the interest of colonial anthropologists, and they invited We'wha to educate them and other white settlers about their culture. But while We'wha themself may have been a source of colonial interest, two-spirit culture was being dismantled by Protestant missionaries, who were sent to assimilate all Indigenous people into white society.

These missionaries used violence to force their binary ideas of gender onto the Zuni people, and lhamana were driven underground. Sacred lines of cultural transmission were severed as a result, and young Zuni people born into colonial America weren't introduced to the spiritual importance of lhamana. Instead, they were brought up under the beliefs of the Christian settlers.

There are very few well-known two-spirit people, because colonial forces turned even their own people against them. However, today lhamana and other two-spirit people are reclaiming what was lost, reconnecting with their sacred ancestors and rewriting their history.

Indigenous peoples of so-called America weren't the only Indigenous peoples to recognise and celebrate gender beyond the binary. Prior to colonisation, a vast number of Indigenous cultures recognised gender diversity in similar ways. Each of these cultures is profoundly unique, with their own rites and beliefs, but there's a common thread across them: they hold those whose gender lies outside the binary in particularly high regard, often as spiritual leaders, teachers and healers.

Prior to Spanish invasion of the Philippines, Indigenous cultures revered a group of healers and cultural leaders known as the babaylan. They presented as women but could be of any sex.

In Hawaii, māhū is a word that roughly translates to 'in the middle' and describes people of a third gender, neither men nor women, who were deeply respected protectors of Hawaiian cultural history. In the Polynesian art form known as the Hula, māhū would perform the roles of sacred goddesses.

In Samoa, fa'afafine are people of a third gender, assigned male at birth but who are chosen (by themselves or others) to occupy feminine cultural roles and whose gender expression can range from the masculine to the feminine. Alongside fa'afafine there is another gender known as fa'afatama, whose sex is female but who take on masculine roles.

The Zapotec people, who are indigenous to Oaxaca in Southern Mexico, use the word muxe to describe their third gender. Prior to Spanish colonisation, and in some places even today, muxes hold a position of respect in Zapotec culture.

And there's a word indigenous to the people of the Tiwi Islands, now part of so-called Australia – yimpininni – that describes people born male but who possess the female spirit and who today might call themselves sistergirls. Yimpininni or sistergirls were not only accepted in their culture, they were considered integral to family life.

There are countless cultures around the world that have had expansive notions of gender for millennia. There is no way of knowing how our understanding of gender might have been different if Europeans hadn't hoisted their flags and headed for the horizon – if Christian missionaries didn't ban Indigenous peoples from practising their cultures, force the Bible upon them and, like they did in many places, take their children to be raised by white families. Severing familial ties meant there was little way for culture to be passed down, and banning the use of Indigenous languages eroded the history of the world's third-gender peoples.

61

Devastatingly, the result is that many once-sacred people have now become stigmatised – even within their own cultures – through the ongoing effects of colonisation.

There's been a lot of recent discussion on social media about intent vs impact, and these god-fearing missionaries are a solid case in point. They were committing these acts with the hope of getting into heaven; if only they had known the phrase 'the road to hell is paved with good intentions'. However, the devastating impact of the missionaries was only one part of the irreparable pain and trauma brought about by colonialism.

So that's the 'god' part, now let's talk about 'gold'.

The second motivation behind the colonial Age of Exploration was, of course, wealth. European powers were keen to expand their empires not just to stroke their egos, but also to profit off the resources of foreign lands. Precious stones, spices and the slave trade held particular appeal. The Europeans would traffic enslaved people from their colonies in Africa to the Americas. There, they would be forced into labour, harvesting natural resources to be shipped back to Europe.

This is one of the darkest periods in human history, and this horrific economy lasted for hundreds of years. Over this period, historians estimate over twelve million enslaved people were forced aboard deadly, overcrowded ships bound for the Americas, and it's estimated that around two million didn't survive the journey.

This number is staggering, but it would be much higher if Indigenous people around the world did not fight back furiously.

Nzinga of Ndongo and Matamba

One leader who fiercely protected her people from enslavement was Ana Nzinga of Ndongo, a kingdom that formed part of modern-day Angola during the seventeenth century. One of the African continent's most powerful and effective rulers, Nzinga protected her people from the expanding slave trade by negotiating with Portuguese colonisers.

To do this, she realised she needed to work with the Portuguese to position Ndongo as an intermediary kingdom, rather than a source for the slave trade. For two years she succeeded, but in 1626 the Portuguese betrayed her, and Nzinga and her people were forced west, conquering the neighbouring kingdom of Matamba.

Nzinga fortified Matamba by welcoming those who managed to outrun enslavers and Portuguese-trained African soldiers. Under Nzinga's reign, the Kingdom of Matamba became a formidable African power, successfully trading with the Portuguese colony until Nzinga's death at age eighty-one.

Nzinga has become a powerful symbol of resistance, not just against colonialism but also against binary gender. She wore only male attire and was widely referred to using the local word for 'king'. This wouldn't have been unusual, as gender in Ndongo and Matamba was fluid. Women could take on masculine roles and become husbands of other women, and men could do the opposite.

Nzinga also kept a sort-of harem made up of over fifty chibados (also known as quimbandas), who were people of a third gender. Chibados were of male sex but presented as women. Like other third-gender peoples we've mentioned, chibados were highly revered and respected prior to colonisation, taking on the roles of spiritual arbiters in the kingdom's political matters.

Ana Nzinga of Ndongo and Matamba is not the only leader who resisted colonisation, but she is definitely worth celebrating as someone who stood in the way of slavery, colonisation and European constructs of gender.

The final motive historians point to for the Age of Exploration is 'glory' – the Europeans sought kudos for expanding their empires as far as possible. That's right: these journeys to colonise distant lands were literal ego trips.

The glory, however, didn't come easy. Crossing the open ocean on a wooden sailing ship was treacherous – there was unpredictable weather, poor-quality maps, dwindling supplies, starvation, disease.

Oh, and pirates.

Pirates were all-male crews – with some exceptions. Anne Bonny and Mary Read were two pirates who eschewed the confines of society and women's clothing in favour of a life at sea. Onboard they both passed as men, but when Bonny realised she was attracted to Read, she revealed her gender. To Bonny's surprise, Read replied that she was also born female, and a queer pirate love story set sail.

THE VERY GAY LIFE OF
Pirates

As you've probably gathered by now, life for most people during the Age of Exploration wasn't very pleasant. But one of the better places to find yourself was on board a pirate ship. The end of the Age of Exploration overlapped with the Golden Age of Piracy, which began in the mid 1600s and lasted until the 1730s.

When pirates attacked, they would steal the loot and commandeer the ship, killing anyone who got in their way. It was a simple, successful formula. They weren't picky about the vessels they chose to attack, and they weren't picky about their crew, either. In fact, pirate ships were radically inclusive compared to life on land. Often (but not always) when pirates attacked slave ships, those on board were able to join the pirate crew. Formerly enslaved crew members were treated relatively equally to the rest of the crew. It wasn't freedom, but on balance, historians believe it was far better than the life that awaited them in the Americas. (It's important to note, however, that the relationship between piracy and slavery is complex. Some pirate crews profited directly from the slave trade while others greatly hampered it.)

Pirate life wasn't just appealing to those seeking freedom from enslavement; the lawlessness of life at sea also attracted the rebellious, the adventurous and the same-sex attracted. As you know, homosexuality was illegal and punished harshly in many places in this time. But pirates were an all-male crew, so to reduce tension on board, men would begin relationships with one another. These relationships weren't a secret, and they weren't just tolerated, they were encouraged, and even formalised in a kind of civil union called a 'matelotage'.

Matelots would do everything together. They would fight side by side and embrace before entering battle. They were also granted inheritance rights – if one matelot died in battle, their possessions and loot would automatically go to the other. Society has taken years to grant these same rights our community, and we're still a long way off in many countries and are fighting to defend them in others.

Matelotage, like marriage, could occur for a range of reasons, not all of them romantic. But we do have records of pirate love stories, like the one between Captain Bartholomew Roberts and George Wilson. Captain Bartholomew Roberts, known on the pirate scene as 'Black Bart', was the most swashbucklingly stylish pirate on the high seas. He was known for wearing a crimson waistcoat and an expensive hat featuring an instantly recognisable red feather, the sight of which caused his targets to surrender almost immediately.

As far as pirate captains go, Roberts was very strict. He kept his crew on a tight leash, reportedly taking a hardline stance against gambling and demanding that lights were out by 8 pm. But Roberts developed a soft spot for the ship's young surgeon, George Wilson. Witnesses at the time attest to the pair's intimacy on board, and they were engaged in a matelotage, pledging to blow up and 'go to hell together' if they were ever captured. Another pirate even alleged that Roberts dressed up in a fresh set of clothes for Wilson, which is nice, because despite being surrounded by water, pirates aren't really known for their cleanliness.

All things considered, the pirate life wasn't perfect, but if you were a queer buccaneer it was gold.

To collect new territories for their empire, colonisers would invade and occupy foreign lands using force, which in places like Australia resulted in the genocide of Indigenous peoples. The colonial government would establish control of the people and implement their laws. The English, and later British, liked to brag that theirs was the 'empire on which the sun never set', meaning they ruled over so many territories around the world that it was always daytime in at least one. And every single one of these cultures would be forced to adhere to British law – including the Buggery Act 1533.

While Indigenous cultures typically had a significantly more fluid concept of gender, many had equally fluid attitudes towards sexuality.

In India, where the majority of the world's Hindus live, pre-colonial notions of sexuality are well documented. Most famously, texts like the *Kama Sutra* show the openness and tolerance in pre-colonial India towards desire. There are chapters in the *Kama Sutra* devoted to homosexual acts with no judgement cast upon them. With regard to gender, other sacred Hindu texts describe a third gender known as tritiya prakriti, which refers to people of male sex with feminine gender expressions.

When the British colonised India, they enacted a version of the Buggery Act 1533, and called it Section 377. This criminalised not just homosexuality, but also any group British authorities considered 'deviant' – including tritiya prakriti.

Today, tritiya prakriti make up part of the transgender, non-binary and intersex community known as hijra, and while they still face extraordinary barriers as a result of colonisation, there have been some steps forward. In 2008, the state of Tamil Nadu recognised a third gender, and in 2018, India finally repealed Section 377. It took 157 years to undo this poisonous colonial law.

All countries that spent time under British colonial rule have had a version of the Buggery Act or Section 377, and in many of them it still stands. In the cruellest irony, since making 'progressive' moves in establishing freedoms and rights for queer and transgender people, the West now all too often look upon the situation of LGBTQ+ people in the Global South with pity – as if the West was somehow not responsible for exporting homophobia and transphobia to these places to begin with.

Let's go back to seventeenth-century New England and follow up with the Puritans, on their mission to spread their austere fundamentalist ways to the New World.

Unsurprisingly, the Puritans were busy making more enemies. Not just the Indigenous people, but other Christian denominations who had begun to arrive.

Quakers, whose take on Christianity was so radical they were heavily persecuted in England, arrived in the New World in the hope of establishing a sanctuary of religious freedoms for their people. The Quakers saw things very differently to the Puritans. They believed that god lived inside everyone and that all people should be treated equally. They were also vocal in campaigning against slavery, which led to their ostracism from society.

When they arrived in New England, the Quakers connected with Indigenous tribes and welcomed their beliefs. While colonial forces were committed to the genocide of Indigenous cultures and lives, Quakers protested against the bloodshed and used their funds to support them. Of course, the Quakers themselves were colonisers, and absolutely contributed to the forced assimilation of Indigenous peoples to a Christian way of life, but their beliefs of freedom and equality meant they were outliers in colonial America – and were profoundly detested by the Puritans.

To the Puritans, the Quakers were terrifying. They used accusations of witchcraft and heresy as grounds to have the Quakers imprisoned, beaten, whipped or hung at the gallows. This persecution drove a group of Quakers towards Rhode Island, where they settled and continued their spiritual work.

The Public Universal Friend

In 1752, a child was born in the colony of Rhode Island. The child – a descendant of the original Quakers – was assigned female at birth and given the name Jemima Wilkinson. The Wilkinsons instilled in their child Quaker beliefs such as prison reform, anti-slavery, teetotalism and plain dress.

In 1776, Wilkinson fell gravely ill with a fever that spread through the colony, believed to have been typhus. Wilkinson's fever ravaged their body for days, and when it broke, they announced that Jemima Wilkinson had died, and they were in fact a preacher who was neither male nor female, and who had been sent by god to inhabit Jemima's body. This genderless preacher would be known only as the Public Universal Friend, or the Friend for short.

The Public Universal Friend adopted an androgynous gender expression, mixing male and female attire, such as skirts and neckties. The Friend wore their hair cropped close to their scalp on top, with long ringlets down the back and sides.

The Public Universal Friend was met with distrust among the community. The Friend's family didn't believe them and took issue with the Friend making themselves unique. Others in the community saw the Friend as either a spectacle or something to be feared.

Yet the Friend was unwavering in their mission. They travelled throughout Northern America preaching god's word, calling for the abolition of slavery and arguing against marriage. They soon attracted a large group of followers, who came to be known as the Society of Universal Friends. Many of these Universal Friends were persuaded by the Friend to free their enslaved people, and a big portion remained unmarried. A particularly large subsection of the Society of Universal Friends were unmarried women, following the Friend's teachings that women ought to obey god, not men.

As the Society of Universal Friends grew, the Friend began to attract criticism from newspapers, and soon noisy crowds would assemble wherever they preached. At the turn of the next century the Friend's health began to decline, and in 1819 the Friend delivered a final sermon before the second death of that body. The event was marked in the society's death book in a single entry that reads: '25 minutes past 2 on the Clock, The Friend went from here'.

After the Friend's death, the Society of Universal Friends continued their service, but over time, the Society also faded into obscurity. The legacy of the Public Universal Friend, however, has not. Throughout history, gender-diverse people have found a kindred spirit in the Friend, who understood that to exist above gendered lines can be sacred.

The Age of Exploration technically ended once permanent colonies and trade routes had been established in Africa and the Americas. However, this 'exploration' continued well into the eighteenth century. From there, the process of colonisation continued, and still continues today. It is embedded in the systems and structures of Western society. Homophobia and transphobia form just one part of its brutal legacy, but these two things have caused irreparable pain to so many people. Decolonisation is a long process that lies ahead and involves everything from land rights and sovereignty to removing colonial constructs from the ways we think about gender and sexuality. In recent years, as awareness about the connection between gender, sexuality and colonisation has grown, queer and trans people of colour have been reconnecting with the history of their ancestors to bring about healing and dismantle the ship built by colonisation.

Next, we'll pick up in eighteenth-century Europe, which was in the throes of the Industrial Revolution. But the only manufacturing we're concerned with is what came out of the rumour mill.

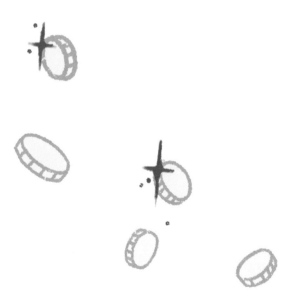

GOD, GOLD AND GLORY

CHAPTER FOUR

Have You Heard the Rumours?

In early 2020, on TikTok, a code evolved among young queer women to help them determine a woman's sexuality. They would ask, 'Do you listen to Girl in Red?' While this Norwegian artist was popular among women-loving women, the question was actually a coded way of asking 'Do you also like girls?'

Versions of this coded question will pop up throughout this book, because let's face it: for large slabs of history, same-sex attracted people have needed a creative, and discreet, way to find out if the person we're into is on our wavelength.

One of the earliest versions of this question concerns the last queen of France, Marie Antoinette. Most people's knowledge about this French monarch is limited to the phrase 'Let them eat cake', which is not only poorly translated from the French 'Qu'ils mangent de la brioche' (brioche is more bread than cake), but also something she probably never said. That said, the phrase does convey the mood of the French people prior to the French Revolution at the end of the eighteenth century.

Marie Antoinette was widely detested, and her lavish lifestyle in the Palace of Versailles was frequently mocked in gossip publications. Journalists loved to write of their queen's promiscuous affairs, especially with two of her close friends, the Princesse de Lamballe and the Duchesse de Polignac. These stories were often accompanied by pornographic illustrations, often featuring large dildos. One such gossip publication went so far as to publish a satirical opera titled 'The Royal Orgy'.

These rumours were spread with the specific goal of slandering the queen's reputation, but there is no evidence to suggest Marie Antoinette didn't have relationships with either the princess or the duchess – there are many accounts of her having devoted and intimate connections with both women. Marie Antoinette struggled to have children as well as to consummate her marriage with her husband, Louis XVI (spare a thought for them; they were both very young teenagers, and no-one deserves to have the weight of an entire kingdom overshadowing their first time). The young Marie Antoinette was lonely, and her female friends were dear companions. We don't know if they were more than that, but as queen she could certainly have maintained an affair if she wanted to – and let's face it, the Palace of Versailles certainly has a lot of rooms.

Whether these rumours were a case of where there's smoke there's fire, or entirely baseless accusations, in the eyes of sapphic women they were canon. So for more than a century, dropping a mention of Marie Antoinette was a veiled hint at your sapphic desires that only similarly inclined women would understand.

Marie Antoinette and her close friend the Duchesse de Polignac appear in a passionate embrace along with the caption, 'I only breathe for you ... a kiss, my beautiful Angel!' If we forget that the purpose of this illustration was to ridicule the French monarch, it would otherwise be a beautiful sapphic scene.

We can't exactly thank Marie Antoinette for this next bit, but the revolution that sent her to the guillotine and ended the French monarchy also had an unexpected outcome for homosexual people.

In 1791, during the French Revolution, a new French constitution was drafted. The French were sick of being ruled by a power that spared not a single care for their wellbeing, so this new constitution excluded all prior laws that had interfered with people's private lives – including those criminalising sodomy. As a result, France became the first European country to decriminalise homosexuality.

To be clear, this didn't mean homosexuality was accepted in France (it was still seen as immoral), but it did mean you couldn't be imprisoned or killed for it, which was a bit of a game-changer. Paris became a covert hub for homosexual people in Europe, and a destination for those fleeing persecution from neighbouring countries. Cruising spots were established and same-sex attracted women experienced growing representation, thanks to the artistic bent of the romantic period.

So by the early nineteenth century, life was improving for same-sex attracted people in France, but in neighbouring England, life was about to get more difficult.

The saving grace of England's Buggery Act 1533 was that it was quite difficult to prosecute, as it required proof that anal penetration had taken place. Given anal sex is typically a fairly private pursuit, it was difficult to prove unless there was a witness. But that didn't stop prosecutors from trying.

Fanny and Stella

Fanny and Stella were two friends, both assigned male at birth, who were part of a British theatre troupe. The theatre already attracted camp, flamboyant individuals, and cross-dressing for the purpose of entertainment was accepted and even enjoyed, but Fanny and Stella were not cross-dressing for the purpose of entertainment. Their effeminate mannerisms and women's dress continued off the stage and onto the streets of central London, where they went about their business and successfully sold plenty of sex.

One spring evening in 1870, Fanny and Stella were leaving London's Strand Theatre wearing women's clothing when they found themselves arrested for 'conspiring and inciting persons to commit an unnatural offence'. They were held on remand awaiting trial, and they were subjected to a string of invasive and scientifically baseless examinations to their anuses and genitals. Prosecutors found that both had elongated penises and easily dilated anuses, which they claimed was evidence of sodomy. The defence brought in more doctors, who all ruled that Fanny and Stella's penises were a perfectly normal length and that there was nothing remarkable about their anuses.

This evidence was shared at the trial, along with testimonies from a line-up of witnesses who all confirmed they had not personally seen any 'impropriety of conduct' from the pair. Disappointingly for the prosecution, Fanny and Stella were released free of charge.

The trial of Fanny and Stella (referred to in the press at the time using their last names, Boulton and Park) wasn't the only trial of this nature to capture the public's attention, but it's of particular note because it ramped up concern over acts of buggery occurring in British society. British parliament felt they needed to combat this 'threat', so in 1885 they updated the Buggery Act to make it more general, and easier to prosecute.

The updated act is known as the Labouchere Amendment 1885, named after the English diplomat who introduced it, Henry Labouchere. It declared 'gross indecency' – which covered off all homosexual conduct between men that fell short of penetrative sex – to be a crime in Britain, and could be used in any case where buggery was hard to prove. The exact behaviours that may have constituted gross indecency were not explicitly listed, which meant the act's interpretation was left up to the courts. In effect, it was a kind of wild card that could be used against suspected homosexuals, meaning they could be imprisoned or sentenced to hard labour on very vague grounds.

As you've probably noticed, the British law only targeted men. There's a common myth that this is because Queen Victoria refused to believe women could ever do 'indecent' things with each other. But as appealing as the thought of lesbian adventures happening right under an ignorant monarch's nose is, that wasn't quite the case.

During the 1800s the British parliament (and Queen Victoria) were absolutely aware of sex between women. Marie Antoinette wasn't the only woman to be publicly accused of having lesbian affairs, and lesbian themes can be found in countless poems and literature of the period. The reason women escaped prosecution for gross indecency can be put down to the way 'respectable' women were perceived at the time.

In Victorian society, women were seen as innocent, desireless and vulnerable to corruption. In nineteenth-century medicine, women with any kind of sexual appetite were treated for 'female hysteria', an affliction with no known cause (probably because it doesn't exist). Given all this, it was deemed best to keep this frightful discussion far from the public forum, lest society's respectable women get ideas. The accepted approach to deal with the threat of lesbianism wasn't prosecution, but silence.

So in refuting the absurdity of Queen Victoria refusing to believe lesbians existed, we are revealing an even more absurd truth: those in charge of Britain were terrified that mentioning lesbianism would make it catch on.

Much later, in the 1920s, the British parliament again became concerned lesbianism was a growing problem, so they sought to have same-sex relations between women added to the 'gross indecency' act. After lengthy (and frankly very funny) parliamentary debate, once again the decision was to leave women out of the legislation, for pretty much the same reason. One MP argued that by banning lesbianism, it 'would be made public to thousands of people that there was this offence; that there was such a horror'. Basically, the parliament feared that banning physical intimacy between women would make more women keen to try it out.

Although lesbians were never prosecuted for gross indecency, they were still persecuted for all sorts of things adjacent to their sexuality, such as cross-dressing and fraud. These cases typically affected women with masculine gender expressions – those who perhaps today might identify as trans men – as well as those who presented male to access the wealth of privileges afforded to men.

Once enshrined in British law, the Labouchere Amendment 1885 was rolled out through the British colonies, from Sudan to Australia, Malaysia and Singapore, destroying countless lives around the world. In more than thirty-five of these places, it still stands.

The most famous person to be convicted of gross indecency under the Labouchere Amendment 1885 was the playwright Oscar Wilde, in a highly publicised trial that changed the course of homosexual history.

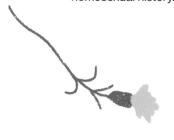

HAVE YOU HEARD THE RUMOURS?

Oscar Wilde

Oscar Wilde, or Oscar Fingal O'Flahertie Wills Wilde if he was in trouble, was born in Dublin in 1854. He was a prolific writer whose literary career covered off every medium you could imagine. He wrote academic papers and criticism, he became a journalist, he edited a women's magazine, he authored lectures on interior design, he wrote fairytales, plays, political essays and prose. What couldn't the man do?

Wilde settled in London, married a woman named Constance Lloyd, had two children named Cyril and Vyvyan, and in 1891 wrote his first and only novel, *The Picture of Dorian Gray*, an ode to youth and beauty. Upon publication it was dismissed as immoral, not just for the hedonism of the characters and their aesthetic sensibilities, but also for its homoerotic themes.

The novel tells the story of a man who is intoxicated by the beauty of a younger man – which proved to be rather prophetic, as not long after the book's release, Wilde found himself utterly transfixed by the poet Lord Alfred Douglas, who Wilde would fondly know as 'Bosie'. Bosie was rich, spoilt, beautiful and sixteen years Wilde's junior. He wrote extensively about same-sex love, evocatively describing it as 'the love that dare not speak its name'.

Bosie and Wilde met their match in one another and began a tumultuous affair that would go on to be the great Oscar Wilde's undoing. Bosie drew Wilde into London's underworld of parties and 'rent boys' – young male sex workers. Many were teenagers of the working class, and Wilde would buy their company in the kind of exploitative relationship we've seen similarly powerful men continue to engage in over recent years.

Oscar Wilde's downfall unfolded, in tragic irony, like the storyline of one of his own plays. Bosie was the son of John Douglas, Marquess of Queensberry, a British (and brutish) nobleman and avid boxer who was disgusted when he heard rumours of his son's affair. When Wilde refused to end the affair, the marquess embarked on a widespread harassment campaign that culminated on Valentine's Day in 1895, at the grand opening of Wilde's best-known work, *The Importance of Being Earnest*, at St James's Theatre in London.

Knowing the upper echelons of society would be in attendance, the marquess purchased a ticket and planned to throw a bouquet of rotting vegetables on stage to humiliate the playwright. However,

Queensberry was barred from entry. This sent him into such a rage that he instead scrawled a message on a calling card that read 'for Oscar Wilde posing sodomite'. (Okay, actually he wrote 'somdomite', but you get the idea – and so did everyone else.) This was a dangerous accusation and a real threat to Wilde's shining reputation, so, in retaliation, Wilde sued his lover's father for libel.

Here's the thing about libel – it doesn't apply if the accusation is true. So Queensberry's defence hired private detectives to investigate Wilde's same-sex liaisons. The detectives persuaded a handful of 'rent boys' to spill about their relationships with Wilde, which was enough to clear Queensberry of all charges and put Oscar Wilde on trial for gross indecency. In a spectacular backfire, Wilde found himself sentenced to prison with two years' hard labour.

After his release, Wilde moved to France, penniless and disgraced, and briefly reunited with Bosie, who had abandoned him throughout both his trial and his time in prison. But their reunion wasn't exactly a redemptive love story – Bosie once again abandoned Wilde after his family threatened to cut him off if the relationship continued.

At rock bottom, Wilde confined himself to his hotel room, where he died on 30 November 1900, three years after his release from prison. Lord Alfred Douglas is often spoken about as the man who ruined Oscar Wilde; this is true, but we would also add Henry Labouchere, the Marquess of Queensberry – and Wilde's own ego.

In 2017, Oscar Wilde was posthumously pardoned of his gross indecency charge, alongside tens of thousands of other men. In the eyes of the law, Wilde is now entirely innocent, but as Wilde's conduct with young boys comes into focus, this innocence has been called into question. Often society's thirst for nostalgia, good news and inspiration leads us to cling on to historical figures like Oscar Wilde as symbols, and in the process forget that they're people. And people are fallible.

HAVE YOU HEARD THE RUMOURS?

As well as being known for his literary works and for the unfortunate scandal that proved his undoing, Wilde contributed greatly to aestheticism, an artistic movement that is best defined by the phrase 'Art for Art's Sake', which basically means that art should be cherished for its aesthetic value over any sociopolitical end. Aesthetes were against the idea that art required a moral or message, instead believing it should set a mood, please the senses or simply exist just to be beautiful. For aesthetes like Wilde, art wasn't confined to gallery walls or poetry collections – instead, all of life could and should count as art, and therefore have aesthetic value. The way a person dressed and behaved, what they chose to read and eat, the relationships they embarked upon – all these things should be beautiful.

Oscar Wilde (left) poses with Bosie in a triumphant display of dandy style. The hats, flowers, waistcoats and walking canes associated with dandies like Bosie and Wilde soon formed a visual checklist for the Western male homosexual archetype.

This 'life as art' approach led to a particular subculture or type of person known as a dandy, of which Oscar Wilde is a notorious example. Flamboyant dress and make-up, charming wit and dedication to their own leisure are all hallmarks of a nineteenth-century dandy. The requirement wasn't necessarily to be rich, but to behave as if one was – a sentiment that continues to re-emerge with trend cycles (looking at you, Anna Delvey).

If you're thinking that these dandies seem a little self-obsessed, you wouldn't be alone, especially if you were around in the Victorian era – a period often defined by its moralism. During his time in the United States in the early 1880s, Oscar Wilde was constantly parodied in the press and caricatured in cartoons for his vanity and egotism. In one cartoon, he is depicted as Narcissus, the Greek mythological figure who was so beautiful he fell in love with his own reflection. This depiction was intended to humiliate Wilde, but to be honest, he probably found it flattering.

Oscar Wilde's celebrity status led society to connect many of the things associated with Wilde – his style, modern painting and writing, the way he wore his hair and his quick wit – with homosexuality. Now everyone was armed with a kind of checklist of things to look out for, forcing homosexual people into secrecy.

The sentencing of Oscar Wilde marked the end of a certain naivety towards queer people. It sent a strong message that deviancy was a serious crime, and set a precedent for its punishment.

When news of Wilde's downfall made its way to Germany, a science-minded man named Magnus Hirschfeld found himself preoccupied with the trial. He believed the kind of 'deviancy' Oscar Wilde was imprisoned for was innate in certain people, and so found himself wrestling with the question of how an element of one's nature could be considered a criminal act.

And look, that's a pretty good question.

CHAPTER FIVE

Through Science to Justice

While conservative morality prevailed in Victorian England, Germany in the nineteenth century was relatively open to liberal ideas. This is because Germany had only just become Germany – prior to 1871, what we now know as Germany was a group of states made up of Germanic peoples, the most dominant being the Kingdom of Prussia.

The unification of these states into modern Germany was driven by the German people opposing an all-powerful monarchy and calling for democracy, in which citizens would have the right to political representation and freedom of speech. This meant that in Germany, ideas that would have been censored by monarchies elsewhere were able to be heard.

Of course, there were limits. The new Germany, like most of Christianised Europe, had an anti-sodomy law enshrined in its penal code called Paragraph 175 (remember this; it will come up again). But there wasn't the same moral panic surrounding its implementation as there was in England, and with Germany's new democratic spirit, one German lawyer was able to come out and petition for its repeal.

Karl Heinrich Ulrichs

Karl Heinrich Ulrichs was born in 1825 in a small town in the Kingdom of Hanover. Growing up, he preferred playing with girls and wearing girls' clothing, and experienced attraction to boys and men.

Ulrichs initially struggled with his desires, but he came to the conclusion that those like him shouldn't be punished, as their desires were part of their nature, not their behaviour.

Wanting to share his ideas with others, Ulrichs (following in the footsteps of numerous same-sex attracted individuals) looked to the Ancient Greeks for the words to describe his feelings. He came up with the German word 'urning', derived from Uranus, the Greek god of the heavens, to describe love between men.

This is considered by most Western historians to be the first word to describe homosexuality as an identity, as opposed to previous words such as 'sodomite', which references an act. Interestingly, Ulrichs understood urning to mean being a member of a third gender, where the spirit of a woman is trapped inside the body of a man. This sounds like what today we might call a transgender identity. Of course, trans identities are far more complex and nuanced than 'a woman trapped in a man's body', but it is worth noting that Karl Heinrich Ulrichs never felt like a 'man', and identified strongly with a 'third gender'. This makes him an iconic figure in transgender history.

Ulrichs would share his ideas about urning identities in pamphlets – like an early kind of zine. He developed his lexicon to include the word 'urningin', to describe women loving women (who he thought to possess a masculine spirit trapped in a woman's body), 'dioning' to describe the heterosexual majority and even 'uranodionism' to describe attraction to both sexes – the first time in European history bisexuality had ever been recognised by name. (While this was novel in Europe, bisexuality had been recognised as the natural way of being in many non-European cultures for a long time prior.) These ideas generated a lot of interest from progressive dionings, as well as deep gratitude from other urnings who, through his ideas, were able to make sense of themselves and their attraction.

In 1867, lawyer and jurist Karl Heinrich Ulrichs did something revolutionary. He made his ideas, and his identity, public. In front of an audience of his legal contemporaries, Ulrichs spoke about the congenital nature of same-sex desire and argued for the repeal of Paragraph 175. There were jeers and heckles of disgust from the audience, but Ulrichs finished his speech and in the process became perhaps the first man in history to publicly out himself. Ulrichs's bravery inspired many people over the nineteenth century, but perhaps most importantly, his admission made him proud. Towards the end his life, he wrote:

Until my dying day I will look back with pride that I found the courage to come face to face in battle against the spectre which for time immemorial has been injecting poison into me and into men of my nature. Many have been driven to suicide because all their happiness in life was tainted. Indeed, I am proud that I found the courage to deal the initial blow to the hydra of public contempt.

It's hard to say whether Lady Gaga was inspired by the work of Karl Heinrich Ulrichs when she released 'Born this Way', but they were definitely barking up the same tree, stating that certain people are simply born with inbuilt attraction to the same sex, and they should be accepted. It's revolutionary to think that this idea was revolutionary two centuries ago, but hey, progress is rarely linear.

Karl Heinrich Ulrichs wrote letters to another homosexual rights pioneer – and another Karl for that matter – Karl Maria Kertbeny. *This* Karl was a Hungarian journalist and dedicated human rights campaigner. He didn't share Ulrichs' view that a man who was attracted to men was a woman's soul trapped in a man's body, or that same-sex attracted men were necessarily feminine at all. Kertbeny used a different word to urning to describe innate same-sex attraction, one that really took off when translated into English: homosexualität, or, you guessed it, homosexuality.

Ulrichs' terminology remained widely used in German, but interestingly, the English translation of urning has come back into use to describe attraction that is inclusive of non-binary people. The word 'uranic' is now used to describe non-femme attraction, or attraction to men, masculine-of-centre and gender-neutral non-binary people.

At the turn of the century, many in the German scientific community had come to see same-sex attraction as less of a criminal issue and instead a scientific or even medical one. Later, this would become a dangerous categorisation, but at the time in Germany it made for a great leap forward. For the first time in history, human sexuality became a legitimate area of scientific inquiry.

There were a number of high-profile thinkers who published their theories on this around the turn of the century – you've probably heard the name Sigmund Freud – but first, let's go back to Magnus Hirschfeld, who was so fascinated by Oscar Wilde's trial. Unlike other prominent physicians at the time, Magnus Hirschfeld was not a politically neutral scientist; he used his scientific understanding as a basis to advocate for the rights of homosexual people.

Magnus Hirschfeld

Magnus Hirschfeld was born in 1868 in the Kingdom of Prussia. He was Jewish, homosexual and a notable member of Berlin's bourgeois elite. Hirschfeld used his connections and social standing to find a sympathetic audience for his theories on sexuality, in particular homosexuality, and founded the world's first homosexual rights organisation in 1897. He called it the Scientific-Humanitarian Committee and its motto was 'Per Scientiam ad Justitiam', which translates to 'Through Science to Justice'.

Hirschfeld believed he could use his scientific expertise to help German society understand that some people are hardwired to be attracted to their own sex. He believed that once people understood that homosexuality was natural and not criminal, the legal reform of Paragraph 175 was possible.

Hirschfeld studied the writing of Karl Heinrich Ulrichs intently and built on it, amplifying his predecessor's thinking. In 1898 – not long after Ulrichs' death – Hirschfeld reprinted Ulrichs' pamphlets. He also wrote many of his own books. As well as using science as a basis for his argument, Hirschfeld, like Oscar Wilde and so many others, also used history. Pointing to figures like Sappho, Socrates, Michelangelo and Shakespeare, all of whom are alleged to have been homosexual, Hirschfeld suggested that if homosexuality was immoral, many of history's greats must also be immoral, and should therefore be removed from their cultural pedestal. Given the book you are reading right now, we feel this is an excellent argument.

It wasn't just homosexuality that interested Magnus Hirschfeld. As well as attraction, he was a pioneer in understanding gender, and delineating between the two. Prior to Hirschfeld's work, most people believed cross-dressing was a kind of symptom of homosexuality, but Hirschfeld noted that many of his patients who cross-dressed were in fact entirely heterosexual. He came up with the term 'transvestite' to describe people whose gender expression differed from their sex, and while this word today is considered by many to be offensive, its development was crucial to understanding transgender people. Hirschfeld believed that gender was a spectrum that ranged from Absolute Man to Absolute Woman. Of course, we now know there is no such thing as an absolute man or woman – Magnus Hirschfeld was essentially using gender stereotypes to categorise people – but among Western European countries, he was the first to articulate how gender exists fluidly outside society's binary boxes.

Science wasn't the only driving force behind Germany's comparatively liberal attitudes towards sex and sexuality. In 1919, Germany entered a transformative new era of government known as the Weimar Republic.

Germany emerged from the First World War with a crippling reparations debt that triggered extreme hyperinflation of the German currency. Newly minted money would lose its value within hours, so the only thing to do was to spend it as quickly as possible. While tragic for the German economy, there is something kind of fun about the idea. People had little choice but to descend into a life of intoxicated hedonism, and many spent their increasingly meaningless papiermarks at Berlin's brand-new cabaret shows.

In the world of cabaret, sex took centre stage, and Berlin quickly gained a reputation for the risqué. If you've seen the 1972 film *Cabaret*, based on gay writer Christopher Isherwood's sojourn in Berlin, you'll know exactly what we mean here. Isherwood was one of many gay and lesbian visitors from across Europe and North America who were drawn to Berlin's alluring nightlife, hustlers, quality drugs and abundant gay bars.

Berlin was also unique for its established lesbian bar scene, which allowed a strong lesbian subculture to thrive. A women's-only night at a bar called Dorian Gray (yet another reference to Oscar Wilde) was a favourite among Berlin's lesbians. The scene grew so much throughout the 1920s that a lesbian bar guide was eventually published, as well as the world's first lesbian magazine, all to help women navigate this burgeoning community.

One of Weimar Berlin's favourite cabaret stars was openly bisexual African American singer and dancer Josephine Baker. She performed as part of Revue Nègre, the success of which tells us about the fetishisation of Black bodies in this time and place. Later, during World War Two, Baker added espionage to her existing triple-threat career by becoming a spy for the French Resistance.

95

Women at these bars established a style of modern androgynous dress that would influence lesbian fashion for decades – hats, tailored trousers, leather ties and a cigar in hand. Women who dressed in this way were known as 'Bubis', which translates to 'Little Boy' but in the context of the lesbian bar scene meant butch. Throughout much of history, masculine women have been seen as anti-fashion, but along the streets of Schöneberg during the 1920s, butch women were all the rage.

In the face of all this hyperinflation-driven hedonism, the Weimar government couldn't exactly hang their hat on the economy, but they could get behind another respected pillar of German society: science. The Weimar Republic came to pride itself on its progressive ideas, philosophy and scientific inquiry, and sexual reform was on the agenda everywhere.

Which brings us back to Magnus Hirschfeld.

Activists from scientific communities were pushing to repeal Paragraph 175, and also for other sexual freedoms like the availability of birth control and the decriminalisation of sex work and abortion. This laid the perfect groundwork for Magnus Hirschfeld's greatest achievement, the Institute for Sexual Science (Institut für Sexualwissenschaft). Founded by Hirschfeld in 1919, the institute was a first-of-its-kind research centre that cemented sexology, or the study of sexuality, as a legitimate academic field. Here, Hirschfeld would build on his work with the Scientific-Humanitarian Committee and advocate for an emerging homosexual minority.

At the Institute for Sexual Science, Hirschfeld pioneered the first hormone replacement therapy, as well as early gender affirmation surgeries. These were monumental, not just as medical advances but because they sought to affirm transgender identities rather than cure them, as many of Hirschfeld's contemporaries argued for.

Hirschfeld worked to have transgender people issued with 'transvestite passes' – kind of like a hall pass for trans people in German society. While cross-dressing or identifying as a gender other than the one you were assigned at birth wasn't illegal, trans people who didn't pass as their gender could be harassed by police for being a public nuisance. Thanks to documentation issued at the Institute for Sexual Science, trans people could go out in German society presenting as their true gender. While admittedly clunky, these passes demonstrate a level of acceptance for transgender people that far surpassed the rest of the world at the time.

Tolerance, however, does not necessarily translate to opportunity, and while society was more progressive, homosexual and transgender people still faced stigma and discrimination, especially when it came to finding work. To counter this, many of Hirschfeld's 'transvestites' were given work within the Institute for Sexual Science.

Throughout the 1920s, the institute set the world standard for research into human gender and sexuality, directly benefiting homosexual and transgender people, as well as cisgender women, for decades after it shut. If it had been able to continue throughout the rest of the twentieth century, we can only imagine how progressed our ideas about the diversity of gender and sexuality might be.

But sadly we will never know, because in 1933, while Magnus Hirschfeld was on a speaking tour, a group of Nazi Youth called the German Student Union looted the Institute for Sexual Science and burnt all the books in the library. They arrived shouting 'Brenne Hirschfeld!' (Burn Hirschfeld!) and set fire to countless volumes of scientific research on gender and sexuality. It was the first major book burning of the Third Reich.

The significance of this cannot be understated, yet so few people are aware of what was lost in these book burnings. Today, it's common to hear people talk about the 'emergence' of transgender identities, like these identities are somehow new. Like there wasn't once a massive library full of research into the spectrum of gender and sexuality that was lost at the hands of one of the greatest evils of the twentieth century.

Being both Jewish and an advocate for homosexuality, Magnus Hirschfeld had enough experience of being persecuted, and even beaten, by the anti-Semitic and homophobic right, to know he could not return to Berlin. He moved to Paris before settling in Nice in Southern France, where he attempted to start anew and set up a new sexology research institute, but he died of a heart attack not long afterwards, on his sixty-seventh birthday.

Hirschfeld was cremated in Nice and his ashes placed in a tomb beneath a slab reading 'Per Scientiam ad Justitiam', an enduring reminder of his belief that through science, justice is possible.

CHAPTER SIX

Welcome to the Secret Society

While the trials of Oscar Wilde pushed Germany forward into an era of sexual exploration, the same events sent shockwaves across Britain and North America. But if Oscar Wilde taught heterosexual society 'what a homosexual looked like', he also taught other homosexuals the same thing.

Wilde would become a kind of symbol or martyr for a collective queer identity, and in the shadows of the criminal underground in Britain and the United States, new communities began to form, typically in low-socioeconomic enclaves like New York's Greenwich Village (which of course is now prohibitively expensive). As these areas were disregarded by those in power, they attracted artists, vagrants, sex workers and other groups society considered unsavoury – making them the perfect place for a secret culture to thrive.

To keep things on the down-low, members needed a stealthy way to communicate with one another. This led to a rich network of secret codes and languages that bound together local queer communities in cities around the world.

Languages develop out of necessity, and the need to communicate without attracting unwanted attention is shared by queer and transgender people around the world. As a result, there are many, many secret queer languages in existence.

In Turkey towards the end of the Ottoman Empire, when LGBTQ+ people were experiencing growing persecution, trans women led the evolution of a queer language called Lubunca. In the 1940s in Greece, a gay language known as Kaliarda (or Kaliarntá) developed.

During the military reign of Brazil in the 1960s, the trans community adopted a language called Pajubá, which incorporated various West African languages into Portuguese. Around the same time, in Apartheid-era South Africa, queer communities of colour spoke a language called Gayle to communicate safely.

In the Philippines, a queer language called Swardspeak emerged during the 1970s when the republic was under martial law. It blended Tagalog, English, Spanish, some Japanese and celebrity names like Janet Jackson and Tom Jones. Swardspeak continues to be spoken by the LGBTQ+ community in the Philippines, but it's now mostly called Bekimon.

And in Morocco, an Arabic-based queer language called Həḍrāt əl-Lwāba has been spoken since the 1980s and continues to shift and evolve with the community.

THE STORY OF
Old London's Secret Gay Language

Given the dark shadow cast by Oscar Wilde's downfall, the gay men of Britain needed a way to communicate without attracting the attention of the authorities. They began adopting the slang used by thieves, sex workers, sailors and travellers, as well as Cockney rhyming slang and backslang (the art of saying words backwards). As London was a major port city, other languages from the Mediterranean found their way into the mix, including French, Italian, Yiddish and Romani.

All this evolved into a fully fledged language known as Polari, a word with roots in the Italian verb 'parlare', meaning to speak. While it continued to be used by thieves, sex workers and travellers, it was the gay community that nurtured Polari, developing it into a wonderfully flamboyant language full of sarcasm, flair and innuendo. In Polari, to ask someone to look, you would say, 'Vada!' To call something lovely, you would say it was dolly, and referring to someone's 'eek' meant their face. ('Face' spelt backwards becomes 'ecaf', which was then abbreviated to 'eek'. Get it?)

The language was abundantly useful. Simply dropping a word in Polari told others you were gay without having to explicitly say so – which would have been a dangerous admission.

As homosexual people gained more freedom in later decades, the need for Polari waned, and the language fell out of use towards the end of the 1960s. However, some words stuck, and the shadow of Polari can still be seen in aspects of Western gay culture.

For example, the words 'camp', 'fairy', 'butch' and 'mince' are all from Polari. As are 'drag', 'slap' (meaning make-up) and 'naff', meaning dull, awful or straight. If you've seen the original series of Queer Eye for the Straight Guy, you may remember one word the Fab Five were particularly partial to: tzuj, or zhoosh, meaning to fix your hair or appearance. They may not have known it, but they were speaking Polari.

There are far too many secret gay argots, lingos, codes and languages to mention, but they have much in common. They evolve during periods of heightened persecution and adopt the lexicons of other historically marginalised and criminalised groups, such as Roma, sex workers, travellers, Jews and thieves. They're often flamboyant, full of innuendo, and lend themselves to gossip. And unlike major languages, which are designed to facilitate widespread communication, these languages are completely unintelligible to all but the few who speak them – which is, of course, the whole point.

It was in these emerging queer communities in Britain and the United States that what we call 'camp culture' began to thrive. 'Camp', meaning 'effeminate' in Polari, describes the ostentatious, exaggerated theatricalities that became synonymous with Western queer life in the early twentieth century.

For many men, life was split down the middle – they had to switch between the heterosexual facade required for public life, and the camp self they became in private. In his monumental work *Gay New York*, historian George Chauncey describes how gay New Yorkers would use the phrase 'letting one's hair down' as a euphemism to describe this unmasking process.

Masquerade balls were the perfect forum for the camp to let their hair down in public. These balls were immensely popular around the turn of the century, and the glamour of them coupled with the anonymity offered by masks was liberating for everyone (not just queer people). Men would attend in extravagant women's dress, and same-sex dancing was encouraged, especially if one of the pair was dressed as a woman. Masquerade balls became something of a Trojan horse for bringing camp culture out from the underground, but the camp community would also hold their own balls. These were known as drag balls, and the guests were history's original drag queens.

THE ORIGINS OF
Coming Out

Today we know the term 'coming out' as a contraction of the phrase 'coming out of the closet', but its original meaning was actually quite different – it referred to the moment a woman was presented to society at a debutante ball. Men adopted the term to describe the moment they were presented to their camp community at a ball – it was all about coming into yourself.

Sadly, this original meaning has been lost over time.

It's difficult to pin down where the 'closet' part came from, but it's thought to be connected to the phrase 'having a skeleton in your closet', which generally refers to a shameful or embarrassing secret. Being gay certainly fit this description for decades, but it is heartening to know that among all the anxiety, and often pressure, that surrounds coming out, another interpretation of the word is available to us. Perhaps we could once again see this defining act not as the unburdening of shame, but instead as an opportunity to introduce ourselves to our community with loving kindness.

The epicentre of these drag balls was Harlem, New York. From 1916, Harlem experienced a huge influx of new residents, thanks to a mass migration of African American people from the Deep South. These people were driven out of their homes by the South's enforced racial segregation laws, and headed north in search of improved opportunities. While there were more legal freedoms in the north, racial prejudice ran deep, so African American people created their own community and opportunities in Harlem. This huge number of people moving into a concentrated area led to an explosion of free thinking, politics, fashion, art, literature and jazz. It lasted throughout the 1920s, and was later dubbed the Harlem Renaissance.

Many leading members of this cultural revival also happened to be homosexual. As a result, Harlem was not only remarkably tolerant of homosexuality, but birthed a great deal of modern Black queer culture. The safety of Harlem drew white gay men from around the city, who would venture north of 110th Street to find community, connection and a wild night out.

This map helped visitors to navigate Harlem's nightlife. On Seventh Avenue, accompanied by a star indicating an all-night venue, is Gladys' Clam Shack, a notoriously gay uptown establishment nicknamed for its resident entertainer – the butch, tuxedo-wearing blues singer and pianist Gladys Bentley.

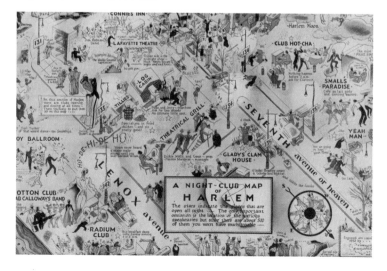

The biggest night of the Harlem calendar was the Masquerade and Civic Ball, held at Hamilton Lodge. The event was colloquially known as the Fairies Ball, so-named for the effeminate gay men who were the belles of the ball. In the 1920s, Hamilton Lodge was one of the only places Black and white, gay and straight guests could all dance together, uninhibited.

Of course, homosexual men made up a decent part of the guest list, but the ball's lively reputation attracted other New Yorkers, too. Heterosexual men often found themselves intoxicated by the 'fairies', 'sissies' and 'pansies' of the ball – those who were so feminine and delicate they passed as women. And the fascination was mutual. The fairies adored being admired, and the heterosexual men didn't feel any shame as these 'women by proxy' didn't threaten their masculinity.

It's worth mentioning here that the terms 'fairy', 'queen' and 'sissy' were empowering labels used to self-identify with a particular brand of hyper femininity. However, they were also used by the heterosexual world as slurs against all homosexual men.

In the period after the First World War, New York was effervescing with a flamboyant new culture, accelerated again by the introduction of Prohibition. As is usually the case, the ban on manufacturing and selling alcohol just made it all the more alluring. Illicit establishments known as speak-easies proliferated throughout the US, thriving alongside the drag balls as places where bootleg alcohol, or moonshine, could be enjoyed in abundance, and traditional social mores were left at the door.

Of course, to operate a speak-easy, the police had to be managed. Organised crime syndicates systematically bribed police to tip off guests about incoming raids, giving them a moment's notice to hide their drinks. After Prohibition ended, these criminal networks would continue to help gay bars operate well into the 1970s.

The mood of the 1920s is best described as complete naughtiness. The formerly respectable New York nightlife had merged with the criminal underground, creating an appetite for all things tawdry and taboo. Both Black and camp culture fit the bill perfectly, and so these formerly denigrated groups suddenly found themselves the height of fashion.

Pansies could be found titillating crowds at speak-easies all over the city, becoming quasi celebrities in the process. Fairies and queens were quite literally thrust onto the public stage, pulling crowds at theatres in Times Square and transforming the district into a camp, hedonistic paradise. While crowds adored the spectacle, it's important not to mistake fascination for acceptance. Newspapers at the time reported on these antics with a combination of disgust and awe, and by the end of the 1920s, society had become completely obsessed. This period became colourfully known as the 'Pansy Craze', and didn't peak until well into the 1930s.

Lesbians also had a moment, with the Pansy Craze accompanied by what's sometimes called the 'Sapphic Craze'.

In Western countries, the early twentieth century was marked by the fight for women's suffrage. During the First World War, a shortage of male workers saw many women going to work in factories. This meant that women were far more visible than ever before, moving out of the home and into public life. When the war ended, people began to agree that if women were intelligent and able enough to work in factories for the good of their country, they were intelligent and able enough to vote for the future of it.

By the 1920s, women's suffrage had extended across the United Kingdom, United States, Australia, New Zealand and much of continental Europe (except France, who didn't get on board until 1944). This was an ongoing process throughout the early twentieth century, but it's important to note that it mostly benefited white women. Indigenous Australians weren't able to vote until the 1960s. Across the United States, some prominent white suffragettes fought against giving African American women the vote, and once African American women *were* given this right, they were subject to an endless list of barriers designed to keep them from exercising it. The 1920s is widely romanticised as a progressive and liberating decade, but this progress was not experienced equally by all.

With their growing workforce participation and political agency, women had entered a new era of freedom – or at least, they felt like they had. They cropped their hair, donned tailored clothing and embraced the persona of a modern woman.

The modern woman was also growing to understand herself as a sexual creature with her own desires – no doubt to the horror of her Victorian mother or grandmother. Over the previous century, it had become entirely accepted that women would have intimate, romantic and dramatic friendships with one another (just girls being girls, et cetera), but now in the twentieth century there was more opportunity to incorporate sexuality into these friendships. And their new lifestyles meant they had plenty of opportunity to meet other women who they desired.

Most of these women didn't identify as lesbians or bisexuals (or 'inverts' – the English-speaking world's answer to urningin and urning), but those who did would soon find themselves the centre of attention.

Fashion took on a distinctly sapphic influence, introducing androgynous dress for women and giving lesbians a way to outwardly express themselves. Newspapers reported on the rise of sapphic attraction, responding to the public's deepening interest in the matter. Even book publishers sought to make the most of the moment.

The year 1928 was a monumental year for lesbian visibility, as a spate of lesbian-themed novels were released in rapid succession. They were not the first to be written, or even published, but they were noteworthy due to the explicit and intimate way they spoke about queer love. These books were published in the knowledge that they would shock – and therefore sell.

What is considered by many to be 'the first lesbian novel' was *The Well of Loneliness* by British author Radclyffe Hall – and yes, it is as dramatic a read as it sounds. The novel is unique because, one, it was written by a lesbian, and two, it explores the lesbian identity, unlike earlier novels written by heterosexual authors, which might have had sapphic moments, but only for the purposes of eroticism and moralising. *The Well of Loneliness* was crucial to the lesbian literary canon. However, it wasn't the first lesbian novel written by a lesbian; it was just the first one written in English.

Radclyffe Hall and her lover Una Vincenzo, Lady Troubridge were part of the elite literary scene during the 1920s, which is well documented in the work of lesbian painter Romaine Brookes. In this painting, Lady Troubridge is depicted wearing a monocle, a lesbian fashion symbol among the wealthy classes.

Nobuko Yoshiya

In 1919, a novel titled *Yaneura no Nishojo* was published in Japan. It tells the story of two college girls who fall in love, and then decide to remain together and make a life with each other. Apologies for the spoiler, but we needed to give away the ending of *that* book because it's important to *this* book – in 1919, a lesbian novel with a happy ending was revolutionary.

Yaneura no Nishojo was written by Nobuko Yoshiya, a Japanese author who wrote prolifically during the Taishō and Shōwa periods. Born in 1896 in Niigata prefecture, Yoshiya would become a pioneer in a genre known as Class S, which centred around romantic friendships between schoolgirls. These stories were full of longing, unrequited love, a distinct lack of dominant male characters and plenty of lesbian subtext, which explains why the genre was popular among sapphic young women.

Class S became popular alongside the rise in all-girls schools after the turn of the century. But most often these stories invoked a trope known as 'gay until graduation', in which the central couple breaks up to pursue marriage or love with a man. In a sense, this was both a blessing and a curse. Love between young women was accepted in society, but only as childish infatuation that was over by marriage. Queer women today have a complex relationship with the genre, which simultaneously celebrates sapphic love while also minimising it.

The Class S genre, however, was seminal in the creation of the Yuri genre, a much more homoerotic extension of these schoolgirl romances that focuses on love and relationships between women. If you've seen *Sailor Moon*, the relationship between Sailor Neptune and Sailor Uranus is an example of a Yuri relationship. (In the US version, this relationship was deemed inappropriate, so they redubbed the characters and made them cousins. Very close cousins.)

Back to Class S. Nobuko Yoshiya wrote many a tragic tale, so *Yaneura no Nishojo* wasn't just unique for its happy ending, but also because it was seen as semi-autobiographical. Through it, Yoshiya revealed her own same-sex attraction.

In 1923, Yoshiya met Monma Chiyo, a mathematics teacher at an all-girls school in Tokyo. Their relationship spanned fifty years, until they were separated by Yoshiya's death in 1973. The two lived and travelled together relatively openly during the period before World War Two. Even though women of her time were required to fill the role of 'good wife, wise mother', Yoshiya never became a wife, and was a mother only in the legal sense.

In 1957, Nobuko Yoshiya adopted Monma Chiyo as her daughter. This was, and still is, the only way those in same-sex relationships in Japan could share property, gain inheritance rights and make medical decisions for each other – the rights that come default with marriage. The practice of adult adoption is ancient in Japan. It's traditionally done for the purpose of preserving family lineage, and in more recent years CEOs have adopted their employees to keep the company within the family. But there are still a small number of same-sex couples who pursue adult adoption as a way to legally protect their relationship.

The Well of Loneliness created such a stir that a British newspaper immediately called for its recall, and Radclyffe Hall and her publisher, Jonathan Cape, found themselves on trial for breaching Britain's Obscene Publications Act of 1857. The book was banned, which may have been a blessing in disguise. Like the book, the trial was high profile and salacious, whipping the media into such a frenzy that in the US – at the height of its Pansy Craze – publishers jumped at the chance to distribute it. These days, someone would win an award for this kind of PR stunt.

The ban in the UK might have appeased certain moralistic reporters, but nearly sixty prominent writers and scientists spoke out against this censorship, even though most thought the book was terribly written. While they didn't succeed in overturning the ban, months later another book was published.

This novel, *Orlando*, was inspired by the family of one of *The Well's* defenders – Vita Sackville-West. *Orlando* was written by Sackville-West's own lover, Virginia Woolf, and tells the story of an aristocratic poet who transitions from man to woman. It's now regarded as a pioneering bisexual and transgender love story.

The options for entertainment were seemingly limitless over the first two decades of the twentieth century. Theatre, cabaret, drag shows, jazz music, literature, newspaper gossip, parties and balls made up the symphony of modern life; it would have been difficult to imagine there could be more to come. But the arrival of 'talkies' – films with sound – was about to change entertainment forever, allowing stories to be shared with a mass audience through the magic of the silver screen.

CHAPTER SEVEN

Meanwhile, in Hollywood

Hollywood's 'Golden Age' lasted from the 1910s until the 1960s, peaking during the 1930s. This was a time of rapid social, cultural and economic transformation, bookended by two world wars, and it all played out on film's brand-new glittering stage.

If you watch a few films from this time, you might be surprised to see certain progressive themes explored. The 1922 film *Manslaughter* featured Hollywood's first ever same-sex kiss. The 1927 silent film *Wings* shows two male soldiers kissing, and film star Greta Garbo kisses her female co-star in the 1933 film *Queen Christina*.

The openness of this period was short-lived – more on that later – but can be somewhat explained by the Great Depression, which was triggered by the stock market crash of 1929. This led to the industrial world's worst ever economic downturn, which lasted until the end of the 1930s. It was a bleak time, with mass unemployment, poverty and skyrocketing suicide rates.

Seems odd that it spurred the growth of a glamorous film industry, right? The thing is, at the time, going to the cinema was one of the few forms of affordable entertainment.

That said, the film industry itself wasn't immune to the impacts of the Depression – it too was being crushed by debt. Hollywood studios needed people to spend what little disposable income they had at the box office, and they knew that provocation sold. Studios deliberately created films with more violence and sexually suggestive scenes in order to get a gasp out of their audience. The people found it thrilling, and welcomed the escape from bleak reality.

The result was an era of film that really pushed the boundaries.

Marlene Dietrich

One face of this progressive wave of film was the Berlin-born actor and singer Marlene Dietrich. In the 1930 film *Morocco*, Dietrich's character dons a tuxedo and top hat and flirts with a woman before kissing her on the lips. The woman blushes and acts coy, while Dietrich's character smiles and confidently flicks her top hat. It's framed as charming rather than deviant, and the woman's reaction suggests the kiss was mutually enjoyed. There was no reason for her attire other than its sex appeal – she wasn't disguising herself as a man to achieve some kind of goal. No, Dietrich was presented as a suited-up woman because the producers knew it would be attractive to men and women alike.

The role married well with Dietrich's life off camera. She was bisexual and part of a group known as the Sewing Circle – a network of sapphic Hollywood stars who all had relationships or affairs with other women (often each other). The Sewing Circle included actress Greta Garbo, playwright and novelist Mercedes de Acosta and French national treasure Edith Piaf, who Dietrich loved dearly.

The Sewing Circle would gather discreetly at each other's houses to socialise away from prying eyes. At the time, actresses would have morality clauses in their contracts, banning all sorts of 'indecent' behaviour, including marriage (it would be indecent for a wife to be a bombshell), falling pregnant (stars who did would be given abortions) and being openly gay or bisexual. (The idea of morality clauses might seem archaic, but recently they've come back into use in the wake of #metoo, to hold Hollywood studio employees and talent to account.)

Despite this, Dietrich was fairly open in her bisexuality and subversion of gender norms. A quote famously attributed to her is 'I am, at heart, a gentleman', though no-one seems to know when or where she said this. She did often talk about her preference for men's trousers, though.

Over the course of her career, which spanned most of the twentieth century, Marlene Dietrich's sartorial choices became wildly popular. Tailoring for women became emblematic of taste and sophistication, and many queer women discovered a new style through which they could express their gender and attraction.

Of course, not everybody was happy about this shift to provocative film making. The Catholic Church, in particular, had quite a lot to say on the matter, expressing serious concerns about the morality of the film industry and pressuring studio executives to do something about it.

The industry responded by introducing a code of practice known as the Motion Picture Production Code. This didn't exactly roll off the tongue, so it became widely known as the Hays Code, after its creator, Will H Hays, chair of the Motion Picture Producers and Distributors of America (another tongue twister). The Hays Code was a set of guidelines stipulating what could and couldn't be shown in film. Ultimately, it was little more than a tokenistic attempt to appease the Catholic Church, and was very rarely enforced. Hollywood continued making films featuring salacious violence and sexually liberated women.

But the Catholic Church became increasingly outraged, and began to galvanise the US Catholic population (a major subset) into pledging to boycott films that the church deemed amoral. The threat of a mass box-office boycott left Hollywood little choice but to enforce the Hays Code.

Things that were forbidden by the code included murder, violence, safe-cracking, nudity, suggestive dancing, 'lustful and prolonged kissing', adultery, childbirth and, troublingly, depictions of 'white slavery'. It also outlawed 'sex perversion, or any inference to it' – in other words, you couldn't so much as mention homosexuality, let alone depict it.

So raunchy same-sex kisses were off the cards. That didn't mean the camp and creative progressives within the industry packed up left. They just had to get smarter.

Writers and directors began to express homosexual themes in a way that would get around the Hays Code and slide under the radar of the church. They would incorporate subtle elements that hinted at homosexuality, leaving secret coded clues, and queer audiences learned to look for these breadcrumbs of representation. This practice became known as queer coding.

Are You a Friend of Dorothy?

If you've seen the 1939 film *The Wizard of Oz*, you might remember the scene where Dorothy meets Scarecrow. She pauses at a fork in the yellow brick road, deciding which route to take, and Scarecrow counsels: 'Of course, some people do go both ways.'

Queer audiences often believe this line is a reference to bisexuality. And this may be why gay men came to use the term 'friend of Dorothy' as a secret code to identify each other.

As a code, it was very effective. If you wanted to know if someone was gay, you would ask them if they were a friend of Dorothy. If they were gay, they'd know what you were asking. If they weren't, they'd have no idea what you were talking about, and you could claim you'd simply mistaken them for someone else. Meanwhile, anyone who overheard would simply assume you had a mutual friend.

There's no real way of knowing the exact origin of phrases like this, but *The Wizard of Oz* has certainly always appealed to LGBTQ+ people. After all, it's about someone who befriends those society considers defective, which is an apt metaphor for how homosexuals were perceived, both by others and themselves.

And then there's the film's star, Judy Garland, who has long been crowned a 'gay icon'. Garland was also in what was called a 'lavender marriage'. During the era of the Hays Code, male gay and bisexual actors would marry a member of the opposite sex to ensure they adhered to the morality clause in their contract. Judy Garland was married to the director of *Meet Me in St Louis*, Vincente Minnelli, who was gay or bisexual. This gave gay men even more of a reason to identify themselves as a friend of Dorothy.

In the next chapter, this story will take a truly mind-boggling twist. It's worth the wait.

To code a character queer, writers and directors would subvert the character's gender to imply homosexuality without making it explicit. A male character could be coded queer by making him effeminate. He might have interests typically associated with women, like clothing and decorating, as well as other traits that were seen as feminine, like delicate gestures and being afraid of things. Over time, this character became a stock character known as 'the sissy'.

On the other side of the gender spectrum, a female character could be coded queer if she was given what society determined to be masculine traits: confidence, a sense of power, a lack of emotion, a loud mouth, strength, crude movements or a lack of manners.

While those enforcing the Hays Code did miss a lot, some queer-coded characters would have raised eyebrows at the Motion Picture Association. However, studios had one other way around this. These queer-coded characters were almost always framed negatively. Male sissies and bumbling masculine women were often a source of ridicule – or they were the villains.

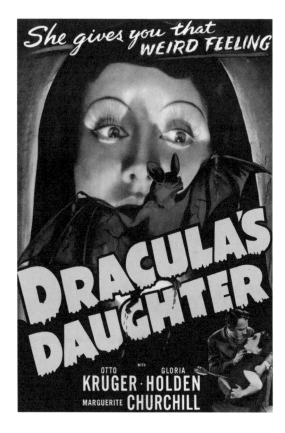

'She gives you that weird feeling.' The poster art for *Dracula's Daughter* (1936) ensuring the lesbian subtext of the film is an easy get.

THE BACKSTORY OF
Film's Queer-Coded Villain

You might have noticed that many of film's classic villains seem a little queer. Hollywood is full of unmarried, childless male villains with impeccable style who commit evil acts with effeminate flair. Female villains have a similar design, but instead of being camp, they are cold.

During the era of the Hays Code, having an evil character defy the norms of their assigned gender was acceptable because surely no moral citizen would aspire to be like them. Not only did they represent immorality, they also usually met a humiliating and untimely end.

In the 1936 horror film *Dracula's Daughter*, the vampiric countess Marya Zaleska is unable to control her thirst for blood. In a storyline that eerily mirrors the conversion therapy used to 'cure' homosexuals, she seeks out a psychiatrist to cure her. Unable to be cured, she falls victim to her desires and begins to prey on beautiful young women. This storyline is so heavily queer-coded that it reads as an out-and-out allegory for the way society viewed lesbians, and helped lay the groundwork for the 'lesbian vampire killer' trope.

In his 1948 film *Rope*, master of suspense Alfred Hitchcock had two male characters commit murder before discussing what they'd done with such perverted excitement it was clearly a metaphor for gay sex. In *Psycho*, Hitchcock had the knife-wielding Norman Bates dress up in women's clothing as he transformed into the eponymous psycho.

The formula worked well, giving enough representation to keep the queer dollar flowing at the box office while skirting the requirements of the Hays Code.

In fact, it worked a little too well. When the code was abandoned in 1968, violence, murder, adultery and lustful (heterosexual) kissing flooded back onto the screen, but depictions of homosexuality remained taboo. Evil characters continued to be queer-coded, creating a blueprint of a villain that became ingrained over time.

No studio adored this character trope more than Disney, which wheels out a queer-coded villain at every opportunity. It gave us the well-spoken and limp-wristed Scar in *The Lion King*, Jafar in *Aladdin* and the outrageously camp Captain Hook, who lives with his life partner Mr Smee. This isn't restricted to male characters; Disney also gave us Maleficent, depicted with a deep, masculine voice, phallic horns and an array of other anti-feminine traits to complement her deep disdain for children. In *The Little Mermaid*, the studio went so far as to base the evil sea-witch Ursula off one of drag's most famous queens – the legendary Divine.

For the better part of the last century, when LGBTQ+ people have looked at a screen they've seen nothing but cold-hearted villains staring back at them. As a community, we've grown accustomed to them, often taking pride in them. However, as Lily Tomlin narrates in the documentary *The Celluloid Closet*, 'Hollywood, that great maker of myths, taught straight people what to think about gay people, and gay people what to think about themselves.'

Sure, baddies can be fun, but some of us are holding out for a hero.

By the mid 1930s the Great Depression was technically over, but the effects were felt up until the very end of the decade – and in some places, into the next one.

One country that was completely obliterated by the events of the 1930s was Germany. The impact of the Depression, on top of Germany's crippling war debt and hyperinflated currency, brought the country to the brink of collapse. German people turned to increasingly extreme politics for answers, and they found them in the far-right ideologies of the National Socialist German Workers' Party, also known as the Nazi Party. By the end of the decade, Adolf Hitler had taken power and whatever limited freedoms homosexual people had previously enjoyed were brought to an abrupt end.

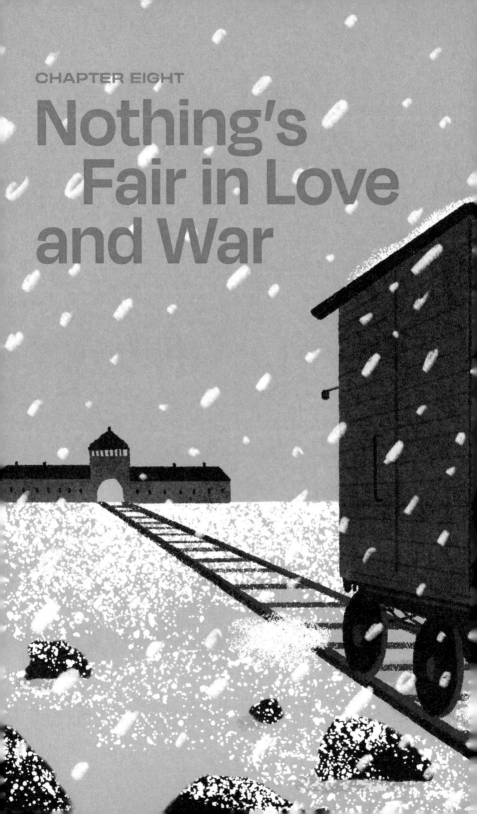

CHAPTER EIGHT

Nothing's Fair in Love and War

This chapter is undoubtedly one of the darkest, both in this book and in history itself. Over the course of the 1930s, the Nazis worked to erase all progressive ideas about sexuality as part of their crusade to racially and culturally cleanse Germany.

Where previously the persecution of homosexual people had primarily been driven by religious doctrine, the Nazis' objection was a little different. They believed that homosexual men were emasculated and weak, therefore would not be useful soldiers in the war effort. Plus, their inability to have children threatened the idea of the pure German family, and meant they couldn't contribute to the establishment of the Aryan master race.

The Nazis didn't just use Paragraph 175 to persecute men accused of homosexuality; they went so far as to redraft it, making it broader and harsher. This allowed the Nazis to arrest men for all kinds of same-sex intimacy, not just the act of penetrative sex.

It's estimated that the Nazis arrested around 100,000 people under Paragraph 175, half of whom were imprisoned, often indefinitely, without trial. As the war went on, many of these men, and a smaller but not insignificant number of lesbian women, would be sent to concentration camps alongside Jews, political prisoners, Roma, Black people, disabled people and many other racial and religious minorities the Nazis deemed inferior. In 1941, Germany invaded the Soviet Union, triggering what the Nazis would call the 'Final Solution' – the systematic murder of European Jews in concentration camps.

There was a strict hierarchy within the camps. Those with higher standing were given far more desirable work, such as supervisor roles and indoor administrative tasks, while those at the bottom were given backbreaking physical labour, subjecting them to exhaustion, cruel treatment, lesser food rations and extreme weather conditions. Most prisoners in that group did not survive the camps.

To enforce the hierarchy, each group of prisoners was classified using a badge system made up of different coloured triangles. Jewish prisoners were forced to wear two yellow triangles, overlapping to make up the yellow Star of David, while other groups were given an inverted coloured triangle.

Because lesbians weren't specifically criminalised under German law, they wore the badge corresponding to the 'official' reason for their arrest. Usually this meant they wore the black inverted triangle for 'asocial' prisoners, or the badge for a racial group they might have belonged to, like Jew or Roma.

Homosexual men, however, had their own badge – the pink inverted triangle. These men were at the bottom of the camp hierarchy. Along with Jewish prisoners, those wearing the pink triangle were deemed the lowest of the low and subjected to the cruellest treatment, not just from the SS guards but from other inmates, too. Of course, it was possible for a prisoner to be both Jewish and homosexual. These individuals were forced to wear a pink inverted triangle atop a yellow triangle, and were treated with particular loathing.

While Jewish and Roma prisoners were being systematically exterminated in gas chambers, the Nazis' approach to homosexuals was neither systematic nor organised. They wanted to 're-educate' or 'cure' homosexual prisoners, and they tried all sorts of things to achieve this aim, including castration, torture and subjecting them to medical 'experiments', which generated absolutely no scientific knowledge. In 1941, guards at Sachsenhausen concentration camp rounded up a group of homosexual prisoners, forced hoses down their throats and left the water running at full pressure until the men drowned.

While these atrocities were occurring, World War Two broke out. Battles were fought all over the world, from Dunkirk to Darwin, and soldiers formed the type of bonds that can only spring from the heightened emotions and hypermasculinity of a wartime environment. Battalions were all men, and sex, love and even romance between soldiers were not uncommon.

In this confronting image, a group of prisoners branded with the pink triangle are marched by Nazi guards through Sachsenhausen concentration camp.

THE STORY OF
Stalag 383

In one German prisoner of war (POW) camp, love between male soldiers didn't just occur, it was relatively accepted. Stalag 383 was a POW camp in Bavaria, and held Allied soldiers who refused to become 'slaves' to Hitler.

Stalag 383 was a former oflag, a camp for officers, so conditions there were much better than in other POW camps. Prisoners slept in small dormitories of around fourteen people and were not sent out to work. They also had comparatively good relationships with their Nazi captors. All in all, life was pretty boring at Stalag 383, and the prisoners found creative ways to pass the time and boost morale.

One group of prisoners established a theatre and put on performances for the other prisoners, with soldiers dressing up in elaborate drag and playing female roles. One performer, known as Don 'Pinky' Smith, played such a convincing woman, he became the camp's pin-up girl.

The productions at Stalag 383 would be considered high end at any community theatre, let alone one at a Nazi POW camp. The soldiers committed to costumes and set design, using what they could find around camp and bartering with the German officers for everything else. The Germans equally enjoyed the productions, often taking up front row seats.

At this camp there were many accepted and loving same-sex relationships among the prisoners, and the camp even changed the sleeping arrangements so all couples could stay together in one block. After the POW camp was liberated, many of these couples were separated, but some continued to write to each other for the rest of their lives.

In a breathtaking display of hypocrisy, there were homosexual men in the SS. Some of these men were put before the SS court while others were allowed to do as they pleased, depending on arbitrary factors like whether they took the active or passive role in anal sex, their Aryan status, and the number and age of their partners.

This issue has become something of a battleground for historians, as while there were certainly instances of homosexuality among the SS, the number has been disproportionately inflated for various political agendas. In Nazi Germany, leftists equated homosexuality with Nazism to deride the Nazis, while today conservatives do the same thing to promote their anti-gay rhetoric. This is an example of how pervasive homophobia is, and of the way homosexual people have had their identities weaponised.

In 1945, when the Allied forces – the United States, Great Britain and the Soviet Union – gained ground across Europe, they encountered concentration camps. Only then did they realise the true extent of the atrocities committed by the Nazis. As the Allies began to liberate the camps, SS guards were either executed on site for their crimes or they fled Germany. Among countless dead bodies, some prisoners were found emaciated but still alive. Many died soon after, but others survived to share the horrors they had witnessed with the world.

Despite living in extraordinary danger, many homosexuals were involved in the anti-Nazi resistance. Willem Arondeus was an openly gay artist who helped create false identity papers for Dutch Jews, and then set fire to the Amsterdam Registry Office to ensure their original documents couldn't be discovered. When Arondeus was captured and sentenced to death, he made it widely known that he was gay and had his friend pronounce, 'Homosexuals are not cowards.'

After the liberation of the camps, Jews and political prisoners were offered financial and moral support in the new German state, which was occupied by Allied forces. But disturbingly, the Allies decided to retain the Nazis' version of Paragraph 175, meaning many of the men who'd been incarcerated in concentration camps for homosexuality were then thrown straight into prison. The rest were shunned by society, and the stigma attached to the pink triangle meant many were unable to return to their families.

While East Germany soon reverted to the pre-Nazi version of Paragraph 175, then stopped enforcing it in 1957 and abolished it in 1968, West Germany, heavily influenced by the Catholic Church, continued to enforce the Nazis' version until 1969, when they rolled it back to allow consensual sex between men aged over twenty-one. Despite all the horrors it sanctioned, Paragraph 175 would remain part of German law in some form until 1994.

They may have been allies during World War Two, but the Western nations and the Soviet Union weren't cut out to be long-term friends. Shortly after the war ended, the relationship did too, over a little thing called communism. The Soviet Union, known as the USSR, wanted to establish communist governments all across Europe, while the Western countries wanted to rid European governments of all communist leanings entirely. A political line was drawn through the centre of Europe, with the democratic West on one side and the communist East on the other – and Germany split in two.

The hostility between the Western democratic and Eastern communist ideologies wasn't confined to Europe. From the end of World War Two in 1945, the United States became deeply suspicious of the USSR, and the tensions between the two nations came to define a period known as the Cold War, which lasted from 1945 right up until 1991.

How Australia's Red Centre Became a Lesbian Hotspot

The Cold War shaped queer history in many ways, but perhaps none more surprising than this one.

In the 1960s, the US government wanted to set up a surveillance facility to spy on foreign missile test launches. The government needed to do this somewhere extremely remote, so spy ships patrolling global waters wouldn't be able to intercept its signal. Somewhere like outback Australia.

Today, the place we call Alice Springs sits on the land of the Arrernte people in a region known as Mparntwe. It's situated right in the centre of Australia, surrounded by remote desert. After Australia was invaded, European settlers established the town as a colonial outpost occupied by men who worked in mining or defence. And in the eyes of the US Central Intelligence Agency (that's right, the CIA), it was the perfect location for their surveillance base.

The facility was called the Joint Defence Space Research Facility, better known as Pine Gap. The public were told it was for 'space research', but behind the gates the CIA, in partnership with Australian spy agencies, was collecting information on Russian missile testing.

You'd be forgiven for assuming Pine Gap wasn't exactly a queer oasis. But once it began operating in 1970, it attracted anti–nuclear war protesters from the global women's peace movement, which in turn attracted a great number of lesbians. In 1983, around 700 women from all over the world attended a peace camp at Pine Gap. The peace camp lasted for two weeks, but many of the women never left.

The lesbians who stayed attracted other lesbians, who found community in this remote desert town, somewhere between Darwin and a top-secret spy base. These days, Alice Springs has one of the largest per-capita lesbian populations in all of Australia.

During the 1950s and 60s, the United States was particularly terrified at the idea of communism in America, so the US government was anxious to ensure that no Soviet or ally could infiltrate American ranks. A senator named Joe McCarthy spread the idea that communists were to be feared, and began investigating anyone with alleged ties to the ideology. Everyday public servants were having to testify before a government panel, answering questions about their political views, who they socialised with, and sometimes being accused of treason.

The US government used a rather bizarre set of criteria to determined who might be engaging with communism. Warning signs included enjoying modern art and having a multicultural group of friends – which frankly makes communism sound excellent! Mostly, these art-appreciative, inclusive individuals weren't communists at all, but many lost their careers, livelihoods and reputations anyway as a result of these investigations.

This period of fear-mongering is known as the Red Scare. It's a widely taught part of US history, and it's formed the basis for many a blockbuster spy movie, but very rarely discussed is the associated moral panic known as the Lavender Scare.

The US government believed that homosexuality was one of the biggest threats to a communism-free America, based on the idea that gay men and lesbians were communist sympathisers or could be easily manipulated by communist spies. There is no evidence to suggest this was the case, but at the time homosexuality was considered a mental illness, and the idea that homosexuals were mentally weak fuelled fears about national security.

Of course, some gay and lesbian Americans were communists – as were plenty of heterosexual Americans – but this was really about conflating two issues the public feared in order to galvanise the US people against a common enemy.

In 1953, President Eisenhower signed Executive Order 10450, which barred homosexual people from working in the federal government, as well as from every government department, agency and private company with a government contract. Executive Order 10450 gave the government the power to investigate and fire anyone believed to be homosexual under the grounds of 'sexual perversion'. Government agents would frequent gay bars and sometimes pose as gay men to expose homosexual employees.

It was even possible to be considered homosexual by association – for example, if you were friends with someone believed to be gay. This meant that gay men and lesbians were stigmatised even further, and driven deeper underground.

During the Lavender Scare, thousands of people were outed and fired from their jobs. Many resigned out of fear, and others took their own lives. While government employees were the focus, gay and lesbian employees were investigated and persecuted across many other industries, including teaching, entertainment and hospitality. These events also deterred many gay and lesbian people from seeking employment, meaning it's impossible to know just how many people were affected.

While McCarthy's Red Scare eased by the 1960s, Executive Order 10450 would continue to keep gay men out of the US military.

THE STORY OF

How Gay Slang Tripped Up the US Military

During the Cold War, the US government, hyper focussed on military intelligence, established the Naval Investigative Service (NIS) to deal with issues of national security and counterintelligence. NIS agents are highly trained in surveillance, forensics and lie detection. But in the 1980s, they would meet their match.

Remember 'friend of Dorothy', the secret code name used by gay men to identify each other? During the 1980s, the NIS was becoming increasingly concerned about gay men infiltrating the US Navy. Through their elite intelligence capabilities, NIS agents got wind that there were many friends of Dorothy in their ranks. They became convinced there was a mysterious woman named Dorothy who was linked to a network of gay sailors, and resolved to track this Dorothy down so they could convince her to talk.

This has been a pretty dark chapter, so let's just pause and acknowledge this. We're talking about the US military. Cracking codes is their thing. Yet even the brightest cryptographers in this elite special service were completely stumped by Dorothy.

The NIS dedicated substantial resources to weeding Dorothy out. Naturally, they never managed to locate her. Perhaps they should have followed the yellow brick road ...

The ban on gay and lesbian people in the military has been longstanding in armies around the world. In the 1990s, many Western countries began repealing these bans, but the US Executive Order 10450 stayed, augmented by the infamous 'Don't Ask, Don't Tell' policy. Under this rule, homosexual people continued to be banned from the US military, but only if they disclosed their sexuality or engaged in homosexual conduct. Unless they witnessed either of these events, military supervisors were prohibited from harassing or investigating personnel.

Don't Ask, Don't Tell was finally repealed by President Barack Obama in 2011, and in 2017, on Obama's last day in office, he signed a complete repeal of Executive Order 10450. It had been in place for over sixty years.

During the early years that queer and transgender people were barred from the armed forces, they were fighting their own enemies – the police.

CHAPTER NINE

Darling, I Want My Gay Rights Now

Today, Pride celebrations occur all over the world and are usually marked by flamboyant dress, dance music, posturing and (eco-friendly) glitter that never leaves your clothes – or your bed sheets. We go to be visible and to celebrate our community, with parties so big they fill stadiums and close down city streets.

It's heady and intoxicating, but if you were to look closely at the crowd, you might spy an older person in their seventies or even eighties reflecting on the fact that these few hundred thousand strangers have all converged in one place to mark the anniversary of a night they were arrested.

In the 1950s and 60s the civil rights movement was transforming US society through activism, showing all oppressed people what social change could look like and how to get there. The success of civil rights leader Martin Luther King Jr's non-violent civil disobedience tactics inspired other groups to advocate for their own rights, and early gay and lesbian groups were taking notes.

In the middle of the twentieth century, homosexuality was seen as a sort of societal virus. Restrictions against its corrupting influence mounted, and homosexual people were essentially excluded from public life.

They couldn't drink alcohol at bars because the US State Liquor Authority deemed them to be inherently disorderly, and bars that did serve this community were frequently raided by the police. Most of the queer world stayed hidden underground, afraid for their jobs and their freedom. Gay men very often married, and their only contact with other men came in the form of clandestine hook-ups in parks or public toilets. Marriage was a necessary part of life for most women – even the gay ones – and though plenty engaged in secret affairs with other women, they remained financially dependent on their husbands.

Butches and transfeminine people of colour faced the most brutal treatment by society and the police. Walking the streets was dangerous, as bashings were common. Trans women who sold sex would frequently go missing. At best, the police would shrug these disappearances off; at worst, they were behind them. So cruel were the police to gender non-conforming people, they enforced a rule requiring people to prove they were wearing three articles of clothing that corresponded to their sex. This rule had no legal basis, but resulted in many LGBTQ+ people being imprisoned, beaten and forced to live on the streets.

During this period, secretive queer groups formed and began to advocate for a better life for themselves. They shunned the word 'homosexual', with its medical connotations, in favour of the term 'homophile'. Two of the most prominent groups of the homophile movement were the Mattachine Society and its lesbian counterpart, the Daughters of Bilitis.

These groups borrowed heavily from the civil rights movement, using the same legal avenues, non-violent demonstrations and community publishing that had proven successful for African American activists.

These groups were assimilationist; they wanted acceptance from mainstream society, so they needed the homophile movement to be seen as respectable. Their protests were conservative, insisting on a proper dress code of a suit and tie, with no cross-dressing or displays of affection. Men would be excluded from the Mattachine Society if they arrived in drag, while the Daughters of Bilitis stipulated that if any member was to wear pants, they must be women's slacks.

Arguably, they needed to be this conservative in order to take even a small step forward, but they also benefited from certain privileges that most other queer and trans people did not. Members were wealthy, mostly white and typically adhered to the roles and clothing of their assigned gender. Black, trans, Latiné, Indigenous, butch, femme, immigrant or poor people would have faced far greater danger advocating for themselves in this way.

A hallmark of the civil rights movement was the sit-in, where activists would peacefully occupy white-only spaces, refusing to leave until their demands were met. Inspired by this, the Mattachine Society decided to host a 'sip-in', to protest laws refusing the service of alcohol to homosexual people. One evening in 1966, members of the New York chapter planned an entirely orderly protest: they would visit a restaurant that had a sign saying 'if you are gay, please go away', declare their sexuality and order a drink. However, when they arrived, the place was closed – a reporter had tipped off the manager. The group tried two other bars, but ironically, this evening both places were happy to have their business, despite their sexuality.

This photograph by *Village Voice* photographer Fred W McDarrah captured the moment the Julius' bartender refused service to the suited-up members of the Mattachine Society in one of the first gay rights demonstrations.

Finally, the Mattachine Society arrived at a tavern in Greenwich Village called Julius', which had begun to attract a gay clientele, a trend the management were trying hard to reverse. The protesters ordered a drink, declared themselves and, as per the laws, the bartender placed his hand over their glass, refusing to serve them.

It sounds like an awful lot of effort to go to just to be refused a drink, but that's exactly what they wanted, as this allowed the activists to form a discrimination case. The State Liquor Authority denied their claims, but soon the Human Rights Commission got involved and it was ruled that homosexual people should be served in bars.

This understated protest was an important step forward that laid the groundwork for future acts of resistance – including one that would happen just a block away, three years later.

In the 1960s, Greenwich Village was still a haven for sex workers, artists, itinerant and LGBTQ+ people, but the police knew exactly where to look if the mood for a raid struck them, as it did on 28 June 1969.

On this hot New York summer evening, inside a mafia-run dive called the Stonewall Inn, people were meeting up with friends or lovers and cooling off with a drink. One young trans woman named Yvonne was celebrating her eighteenth birthday. In the early hours of the morning the vice squad stormed the venue and began arresting patrons, just like they had done countless times. This time, however, there was resistance.

Accounts vary, but multiple sources say that police tried to arrest a butch lesbian who fought back, setting off a riot. The instigator is often said to have been Stormé DeLarverie, who certainly did resist arrest that evening, but whether she's the one who kicked things off is pure conjecture. We love an inciting incident and a digestible narrative, which is why so much coverage about this night is preoccupied with who threw the first brick, or bottle, or punch.

What we do know is that police matched this resistance with brutality, throwing people into police vans – including Yvonne, whose birthday had taken a terrifying turn. But word spread to people of the Village faster than the police could radio for back-up, and police were soon forced to barricade themselves inside the Stonewall while people of all genders, sexualities, races and classes united against the violence of the state.

The events of this evening and those that followed are known collectively as the Stonewall Uprising.

KNOW YOUR ICONS
Stormé DeLarverie

Stormé DeLarverie wasn't just a regular at the Stonewall Inn; she was a guardian angel of Greenwich Village too. Stormé was born in New Orleans to an African American mother and a white father. She spent most of her life moving between two worlds, first by straddling the racial divide in the South and then later moving between the masculine and feminine in a way that even today continues to cause arguments about her pronouns on Twitter. (In this context we have taken our lead in using 'she' and 'her' pronouns from her friend, and later guardian and advocate, Lisa Cannistraci.)

Growing up, Stormé's biracial identity caused her a lot of pain. In the 1920s, biracial marriages were illegal, so Stormé's very existence was taboo. She wasn't given a birth certificate, and grew up with a foster family. Her early life was marked by violence from both Black and white children, and one incident left her hanging from a fence by her leg, giving her a permanent limp. She had a talent for singing, and when she left home she pursued a career in show business, singing in jazz bands. She initially performed presenting as a woman, as we can see from glamorous headshots of the time, but at some point she began performing as a man.

In the 1940s, Stormé moved to Chicago where she presented

male, passing as a straight man. During this period she apparently worked as a bodyguard for the mafia. They were criminals, but so was Stormé, in the eyes of the law. It was there in the underworld that she found her signature attire: the zoot suit.

Stormé moved to New York and joined a drag cabaret called the Jewel Box Revue in Harlem in the mid 1950s. It was the only racially integrated show at the time. Flyers for the show promised '25 men and 1 girl', and audiences were delighted when, at the show's finale, the 'girl' was revealed to be the sole dapper baritone: Stormé DeLarverie in the zoot suit.

Artists and photographers were captivated by this enigma who passed entirely as a man yet would happily be referred to as a 'lady'. Documentary photographer Diane Arbus famously captured Stormé in a photograph titled 'Miss Stormé DeLarverie, the Lady Who Appears to be a Gentleman'.

Male impersonators and drag kings had existed throughout history and were not necessarily tied to 'queerness'. Their masculinity was performative, and so neither label was really apt for Stormé, whose own masculinity remained unchanged as she moved between the streets and the stage. Transgender identities were yet to be discussed, and terms like 'genderqueer' and 'non-binary' were decades off. Given this, the term that probably best captures Stormé's essence is 'genderfuck'.

Shortly after that night at Stonewall, Stormé quit the Jewel Box Revue and once again became a bodyguard. She spent evenings working security at the Cubbyhole, one of the Village's most iconic lesbian bars. It was here that Stormé met Lisa Cannistraci, who went on to take over the Cubbyhole, turning it into Henrietta Hudson, which, at the time of writing, continues to survive against all odds. (The 1970s was a heyday for lesbian bars, which have been dwindling ever since.)

Stormé continued to work security and watch over the Village until she was deep into her eighties. At the end of her life, despite suffering dementia, Stormé's memories of Stonewall were not cloudy in the slightest, and she spoke about that night until she eventually passed away in 2014, aged ninety-three.

Stormé DeLarverie continues to fuck with society's concept of gender. The discourse and debate surrounding her pronouns and gender identity put the 'storm' in Stormé, which is just part of her magic. She never spoke on the record about pronouns or gender identity, but according to those who knew her, when the question was asked, she would reply that she was happy with whatever pronouns made the person asking feel comfortable. This is a solid reminder that gender is much more than pronouns.

That first night at Stonewall marked a shift in the energy of the Village. Protesters returned the next night and again clashed violently with police. The aftershocks from Stonewall continued for days, with more protests breaking out.

Activists seized the momentum in the immediate aftermath of the uprising and formed the Gay Liberation Front (GLF), a union of gay and lesbian activists. Those involved in the GLF were sick and tired of being treated like cockroaches and were determined to fight back. Most of the fighting was done by those who lived on the streets, who were the most marginalised, and were so seasoned with beatings they had nothing left to lose.

What unfolded on the night of Stonewall wasn't unique. Butches and queens had fought back against police brutality before. But just as Rosa Parks became a symbol of the civil rights movement, Stonewall ignited a unified movement towards gay liberation. The Daughters of Bilitis and the Mattachine Society became part of the Gay Liberation Front and finally everyone was moving towards the same goal.

To mark the anniversary of the Stonewall Uprising, a march through the Village was planned. The event was named the 'Christopher Street Liberation Day'. This event became annual – we now know it as 'Pride'.

KNOW YOUR ICONS
Marsha P Johnson

If Greenwich Village had a guardian angel in Stormé DeLarverie, then it had an unofficial mayor in Marsha P Johnson.

Marsha P Johnson (the 'P' stood for 'Pay it no mind') was a Black, disabled trans woman and a prominent Greenwich Village regular, whose warm and welcoming nature drew people into her orbit. Assigned male at her birth in New Jersey in 1945, Marsha began wearing dresses from five years old, until she was forced to stop due to bullying. However, once she had her high school diploma, she packed a bag and moved to New York City.

Marsha lived before the term 'transgender' had really emerged, so during her lifetime she used the terms 'transvestite' and 'drag queen' or 'street queen' to describe herself.

Marsha always said she wasn't a serious drag queen, because she couldn't afford to take drag seriously. She didn't have the money for expensive dresses, shoes or quality wigs like other, mostly white, queens did. Plus, her drag wasn't a perfected performance for an audience – it was her daily life. When she did perform, it was part of a drag troupe called Hot Peaches, and it was more camp, comedic and political than anything resembling the elegant pageantry of earlier drag.

Marsha wasn't trying to pass as a woman, and wasn't afraid of expressing her masculinity alongside her femininity. She used beer cans as hair rollers, and thrifted dresses where she could. She'd find frocks and accessories in trash cans, taking them home to launder and fix up.

DARLING, I WANT MY GAY RIGHTS NOW

Flower crowns were her signature. Marsha spent most of her life without a fixed address, spending many nights on the streets. For a time, she took refuge under tables in Manhattan's Flower District, and was sometimes given leftover flowers, which she would arrange in a triumphant crown. Marsha would often spend her last $10 on a bouquet of flowers, bring them home and delightedly place them in her hair.

She was an optimist, certain she would find herself a rich husband one day and use that money to repay all those who helped her. Although she was radical on many fronts, Marsha also had a conservative streak. She was devout in her religious beliefs, and adamant that sex shouldn't occur before marriage. There was a determined innocence about her, which may have helped her stare down the injustices life dealt her. She spent much of her time on the Christopher Street Pier, selling sex and using the money she earned to help others on the streets. While sex work may seem in conflict with her religious beliefs, it was one of the few earning options for trans women. She was good at it, and soon realised that her body had value.

Marsha arrived at the Stonewall Inn around 2 am on that night in 1969. She was instrumental in the uprising – penniless and homeless with a string of prior arrests, she had nothing to lose, and so was a formidable force. Many witnesses recall seeing Marsha on top of a lamp post that night, throwing a brick through the windshield of a police car.

In the aftermath, Marsha led the drag queen caucus of the Gay Liberation Front, and would remain a key figure in the fight for gay liberation for years to come. A few years later, at a protest, a reporter asked Marsha what the protest was about. Her reply? 'Darling, I want my gay rights now.'

Something that is often left out of Marsha's story is that she was disabled, living with both physical and psychiatric disabilities, as well as addiction issues and, later, HIV. Towards the end of her life her health was declining, so when her body was found floating in the Hudson River in 1992, the police barely cracked a notebook, citing her disabilities as proof of her suicide. However, not one person who knew her entertained the notion that Marsha took her own life. The community was resolute that her death was either a tragic accident or a brutal murder, and that her life was worthy of an investigation.

Calls for the reopening (or opening, even) of Marsha's case continue, as does the fight for the protection of all Black, trans, disabled and queer lives.

After the monumental first Christopher Street Liberation Day, the Gay Liberation Front grew large and unwieldy. Like a runaway freight train, the movement plunged forward. It was making headway, but many of its passengers feared it was veering off course.

Many members of the GLF were also part of other movements, including the peace movement, the women's movement, the student movement, socialism and the Black Power movement. Given the contribution of Black gay men, lesbians and drag queens to the formation of the Gay Liberation Front, in 1970 the GLF announced its solidarity with all other movements fighting against a shared oppressor, including the Black Panther Party, another group working to fight police violence. This caused a lot of division within the GLF, as the Black Panther Party had previously been seen as homophobic, or at the very least apathetic to struggles of gay and lesbian people. However, in 1970 they sought solidarity, and Huey P Newton, the leader of the Panthers, made a momentous call for the Black Power movement to unite with the gay liberation movement and the women's movement 'in a revolutionary fashion' and challenge their own biases towards homosexuality.

Despite this, factions within the Gay Liberation Front still felt the movement had lost its way. Now with chapters all across the United States, the GLF began to splinter as different, more marginalised members like lesbians and people of colour began to focus on integrating gay and lesbian issues into other movements.

Lesbians, who were struggling to have their voices heard over those of gay male activists, shifted their focus to bringing lesbian visibility into the women's movement. This was threatening to some Second Wave feminists, including Betty Friedan, author of the book that galvanised a generation of dissatisfied housewives, *The Feminine Mystique*. Betty believed that lesbian rights were a step too far, made a mockery of what women had achieved (even though they had lesbians to thank for a lot of those achievements) and painted all feminists as man-haters.

Betty Friedan coined a term for this problem: the Lavender Menace. And like any good societal menace would, these sapphic women took that ill-intended title and put it on T-shirts.

To protest the complete lack of lesbian representation in mainstream feminism, these lesbians, wearing their Lavender Menace T-shirts, showed up at the National Organization for Women's Second Congress to Unite Women. They switched off the lights, cut the mic and handed out copies of a ten-page manifesto titled the 'Woman-identified Woman'. The author's by-line read 'Radicalesbians', which was what this group of activists called themselves: Radicalesbians – no space – to emphasise the importance of unity and solidarity within the women's movement. What we now call radical lesbian feminism was born.

The Lavender Menace protest, with their mimeographed manifesto and screen-printed tees, is a prime example of a tactic popularised by another group that rose out of the ashes of the Gay Liberation Front: the Gay Activists Alliance (GAA). This group of gay men and lesbians split off from the GLF to focus solely on gay and lesbian issues, determined not to be 'distracted' by other causes.

While the GLF had a distinct left-wing stance, the GAA declared themselves politically neutral, concerned only with the stance of individual politicians towards homosexuals. The GAA were very effective, and soon this group became the major activist group in the gay liberation movement. This was largely thanks to a direct-action tactic they perfected and named a 'zap'.

A typical zap involved a guerrilla-style demonstration that disrupted the order of a public event or space. They were non-violent events, though one did involve throwing a pie in the face of an anti-gay activist during a press conference. Zaps could take many forms, including mass kiss-ins, staged same-sex marriages, infiltration of conservative events or just generally being present and annoying in homophobic spaces. A good zap was noisy, theatrical and, like the activists behind it, camp as hell.

The GAA were making incredible progress, but soon familiar cracks would appear. Once again, lesbians were struggling to be heard among the men, and once again, they split off from the GAA to form Lesbian Feminist Liberation, leaving the GAA and the broader gay liberation movement overwhelmingly concerned with the challenges of white, middle-class gay men. And while transvestites and drag queens worked alongside the GAA and were often placed in the centre of zaps, when the press arrived, they were always ushered to the margins.

A founding member of the Lavender Menace
was the lesbian feminist poet Rita Mae Brown,
whose poem 'Sappho's Reply' contains the line
'An army of lovers shall not fall'.

DARLING, I WANT MY GAY RIGHTS NOW

Sylvia Rivera

In 1973 at the annual Christopher Street Liberation Day event, a Puerto Rican trans woman and street queen burst onto the stage and interrupted proceedings. 'Y'all better quiet down,' she yelled into the microphone, to boos and jeers from the crowd. 'Have you ever been beaten up and raped in jail?' she screamed.

Her name was Sylvia Rivera and she was talking about her gay and transgender brothers and sisters in prison (remember, cross-dressing and homosexuality were crimes in the United States in 1973, and many were left to languish in the prison system). Sylvia was furious because neither the gay liberation movement nor the women's movement were doing anything to help those imprisoned for actions that served gay liberation.

'I have been beaten,' she went on. 'I have had my nose broken. I have been thrown in jail. I have lost my job. I have lost my apartment for gay liberation and you all treat me this way? What the fuck's wrong with y'all?'

Sylvia's explosive speech, and her very presence, was the embodiment of everything the gay liberation movement wanted to ignore – that their entire movement was owed to the actions of people like her.

Sylvia was born in New York in 1951, and was raised from the age of two by her grandmother, who exiled her from home after she began wearing make-up. By just ten years old, Sylvia was living on the streets of New York City and selling sex to survive. She found community among the drag queens of the Christopher Street Pier, who gave her the name Sylvia. Not long afterward, she met Marsha P Johnson, who was just seventeen at the time. Marsha taught her to apply make-up, and would go on to become her closest friend.

In the aftermath of Stonewall, it was Sylvia who led the Gay Liberation Front with Marsha, concerned for the welfare of their community's most vulnerable. Together, they founded an organisation called Street Transvestite Action Revolutionaries (STAR), which provided housing and support for gay and transgender people who were homeless, disabled or recently imprisoned. This organisation was undoubtedly the most radical and inclusive within the entire movement. The word 'intersectionality' is often used today, and while it wasn't in circulation at the time, Sylvia and Marsha are possibly two of the greatest examples of what intersectionality looks like.

Sylvia was out of town when she received news of Marsha's passing. Like so many people, Sylvia never believed her friend took her own life. Devastated, she moved back to live in the 'gay camp' at the Christopher Street Pier, where she was a mainstay until 1996 when the Hudson River Waterfront Project was approved. The project included removing anything 'unsightly' from the area: the Christopher Street camps had to go.

Sylvia Rivera remained angry her whole life at being continually marginalised within her community. Her rage was necessary – too often those who put the most on the line for change are denied the rewards. In Sylvia's words (as quoted by queer historian Michael Bronski), 'Hell hath no fury like a drag queen scorned.'

If there's one thing we should take away from this series of events, it's the lengths people will go to in order to protect freedoms they've had to fight for, even if that means perpetuating the very exclusion they fought against. Gay men, excluded from society, fought bravely for their freedoms and then excluded those who were poor, non-white, in drag or female. Women, fighting to be taken seriously, feared lesbians would make a mockery of them. Lesbians, excluded from both the women's movement and the gay liberation movement, protected what *they'd* built like a fortress, excluding bisexual women, trans women and sex workers. And though here they form the end of the line, we owe really everything to trans sex workers like Marsha P Johnson and Sylvia Rivera. It's an undeniable pattern: the excluded exclude. It's something we continue to face as a community; today, it's called gatekeeping.

By the mid 1970s, all these activist groups had spawned counterparts around the world. These international groups had the benefit of learning from the US movement and were able to apply what worked to the issues they faced locally.

Life for queer and trans people looked different depending on how their government categorised it: legally or medically. On one hand, life might be marginally safer if homosexuality was seen as an illness, because an illness can't be helped, and therefore shouldn't be punished. Then again, it was arguably better for homosexuality to be seen as a crime because in many cases, worse than any punishment that could be meted out was the prospect of a cure.

In Australia, dances and parties brought activists together, but police harassment was a frequent occurrence – as it was during the event advertised on this poster.

In Australia, the psychiatry industry said homosexuality should be treated as a mental illness. Homosexual people would still be arrested, but they could often have their sentences reduced or commuted if they submitted to treatment. Such 'treatments' would involve aversion therapy – a horrific process where a person would be given drugs to induce nausea and vomiting before being shown photos of their lovers in an attempt to rewire their brain, replacing love with disgust. Sometimes, they resorted to brain surgery.

Traditional lobotomies had fallen out of favour by then, but psychosurgery was common in the 1970s, particularly if you were a lesbian. Lesbians were often forced to undergo an amygdalotomy, which involved the removal of part or all of the amygdala (a pretty important part of the brain) in order to cure a patient's attraction. In the early 1970s, one Sydney hospital was responsible for performing two amygdalotomies a week on lesbians, under the knife of a Dr Harry Bailey. To protest Bailey's butchery of the community, activists dumped a bucket of bloody sheep's brains in the foyer of his offices.

Activists in Australia were in close contact with their international counterparts, and took inspiration from actions overseas. But solidarity and unity was a given; with just a fraction of the US population, numbers were everything. Members of the gay liberation movement would also be present at women's demonstrations, anti-war demonstrations and anti-capitalist demonstrations. They were all in it together.

If the movie *Mean Girls* had been about 1970s activists, one character would have proclaimed, 'On Saturdays, we wear combat boots.' Weekly protests were routine for the angry and idealistic, but they were anything but mundane. Demonstrations frequently escalated to police violence and arrests, but also featured dancing and celebration. Gay and lesbian people were determined to match hatred and violence with pride and fun.

In 1978, US-based activists reached out to the international community requesting solidarity action as part of their Christopher Street Liberation Day plans. In Australia, an organisation called Campaign Against Moral Persecution (CAMP) agreed to hold a solidarity protest in Sydney, followed by a celebratory parade. A permit was issued for the event, the protest went smoothly and the community was looking forward to the evening's celebration.

But it soon became clear that despite granting a permit for the event, the police were not in the mood to party. They began to urge the parade on, pushing the revellers to move swiftly through the streets of Sydney. Many believe what came next was because the police couldn't stand the sight of gay and lesbian people celebrating themselves. Peaceful picketing may have been one thing, but pride was a bridge too far.

The police confiscated the truck and stereo at the head of the parade, shifting the buoyant mood to one of anger and uncertainty. As the group made their way towards Kings Cross, the police began beating and arresting people. In the ensuing days the media released the names and occupations of all those arrested. Many lost their jobs, their families, their rental tenancies. Some died by suicide.

The cruelty that occurred that night left a vicious scar on the lives of lesbian, bisexual, gay and transgender people in Australia, but it did change something. Just like the Stonewall Uprising stirred the people of New York, the event triggered a stream of protests (and a fair few more arrests) that gathered momentum across Sydney, and eventually resulted in most of the charges being dropped. The following year, the community braced themselves for a repeat of 1978, but their carefully collected bail fund remained untouched. The parade was peaceful and these brave activists celebrated what came to be known as the second Sydney Mardi Gras.

The political element of the Sydney Mardi Gras was soon overtaken by the party focus, reflected in the decision to hold future events in summer. After all, a chilly Australian winter didn't provide much of a backdrop for celebration. The shift drew criticism from some people who believed the event had forsaken its protest roots.

Pride marches around the world have had to contend with this concern – that the radical origins of Pride have been obscured behind the facade of a party. Come Pride season, it's important to remember who fought for our right to party, but also remember that for queer and trans people, partying will always be political.

Australian gay and lesbian activists at the morning march held on 24 June 1978 in commemoration of the Stonewall Uprising. Look closely at the flag in the foreground and you'll recognise a pink inverted triangle. It might seem perverse that this Nazi hate symbol would be waved around by a young child among smiling gay and lesbian activists, but the pink triangle was reclaimed by the community as a symbol of resilience and in Australia was the primary symbol of LGBTQ+ pride until the mid 1990s, when the rainbow took over.

CHAPTER TEN

It's in Vogue

Queer and trans people know how transformative the night can be. The expectations of a society in daylight fall away and we can take on new identities, or take them off. Throughout history, queer and transgender people have found liberation and love in the night-time, but in the 1970s all of this would unfold on the dance floors of sweaty underground nightclubs heaving with the sound of disco.

There's a term called 'white flight', which describes the mass exodus of white middle-class Americans from areas with growing racial diversity. This happened in New York during the 1970s, when middle-class New Yorkers up and left the city seeking better job prospects and an escape from the riots, strikes and demonstrations of the 60s.

Their exodus gutted the city of tax revenue, resulting in cuts to the already paltry social services and housing. As the wealthy pursued a cushy life in the suburbs, those who stayed tried to make do with even less than they'd ever had. Those who were queer, Black, Latiné or transgender bound together for safety, and looked after each other in a way the city did not. And they did so with disco.

To use an English teacher's favourite word, the disco phenomenon was really about the *juxtaposition* between a dirty and destitute city and a culture of glamour, hedonism and music. It was a salve to a wounded city, and was driven by those whose wounds were the deepest. At secret underground parties, Black, queer and transgender communities began blending soul music with synthesisers, repetitive beats, funk-driven basslines and uplifting, empowering lyrics. On these dance floors, queer and trans people were able to swap shame for self-love and self-expression.

As they nailed this new sound, DJs brought it out of the parties and into other public forums like gay clubs and bathhouses. Inside the walls of the Continental Baths, a frequently raided gay bathhouse that promised to bring back the 'Glory of Ancient Rome' (refer to earlier chapters for a refresher on this glory), openly gay DJs would match beats and mix tracks, bringing another layer of euphoria to this legendary house of hook-ups.

And they were onto something. The Black, queer and trans community showed the rest of New York how to escape to paradise during hard times. In the wreckage of this near-bankrupt city, disco brought people to life.

Disco fever set in everywhere – even in the suburbs. Across the world, all eyes were on New York, and especially on Studio 54, possibly the most famous nightclub of all time. Most people know Studio 54 for its celebrity clientele, including Andy Warhol, Cher, Diana Ross, Mick Jagger and a young Drew Barrymore. Its reputation for hedonism, endless sex, mountains of cocaine and decadent costumes made it a popular theme for fancy dress parties. But it was, first and foremost, queer.

161

Studio 54 drew its success from the gay club culture it was based on, but it soon began to attract a growing middle-class, heterosexual 'after work' crowd. Of all the establishments of the era, Studio 54 was unique in seeing this as a problem. The owners knew that it was its queer and transgender clientele that made the nightclub special – if it opened to just anyone, the club might lose its cool factor.

To protect their freaky utopia, they developed their infamous door policy, granting people access based on their style or celebrity status, barring polyester shirts (adored by corporate America at the time) and ensuring that at least 20 per cent of the clientele on any given night were gay men and at least 10 per cent were transvestites and lesbians. Sure, it wasn't perfect, but it was certainly progressive. Remember, being openly gay was still illegal at the time.

Early in the disco craze, the gay men, drag queens and trans women who created disco attracted some attention. They offered the kind of edgy escapism adventurous people craved, so again for a hot minute gay was good.

Studio 54 was an incubator for the first generation of queer rock stars. Elton John, Freddie Mercury and David Bowie were regular fixtures at 54 and went on to show the world that their queerness could be part of their star quality. The conservative music industry wasn't quite ready for a strictly gay artist, but there was something fresh about an enigmatic rock star with a fluid sexuality and gender expression.

In 1976, Elton John, Freddie Mercury and David Bowie all came out as bisexual, although it's important to note that the way their bisexuality was framed was not without its problems. These stars opened the door for many people to discover their sexuality, but the media coverage contributed to myths about bisexuality, such as that it's a stopover on the way to gay, or that it's inherently tied to sexual promiscuity.

Art, too, was bringing queer sexuality out into the open. Perhaps Studio 54's greatest legacy lies in the work of Andy Warhol, who used 54 as a source of both inspiration and networking. Warhol, who tends to be more widely associated with soup than queerness, would photograph nude men, turning their bodies into art that feels reminiscent of Michelangelo's work during the Renaissance.

He was also captivated by drag queens, famously sending his entourage to the Gilded Grape, one of the few trans-friendly nightclubs, to find models for him to photograph as part of a series titled *Ladies and Gentlemen*. The women were left nameless, though if you look at the series you'll see the undeniable face of Marsha P Johnson grinning back at you.

In 1968 cult documentary *The Queen*, Andy Warhol can be seen judging the Miss All-America Camp Beauty Pageant. Among the overwhelmingly white contestants is a Black queen named Crystal LaBeija, whose rage at the end of the documentary highlights the injustices faced by Black and Latiné drag queens.

Although New York's drag scene had its roots in the Harlem Renaissance, by the 1960s it was white queens who were consistently favoured in competitions. Black and Latiné queens felt they no longer had a place, so Crystal and another queen, Lottie LaBeija, decided to host their own ball specifically for Black queens.

The event was billed as 'Crystal & Lottie LaBeija presents the first annual House of LaBeija Ball at Up the Downstairs Case on West 115th Street & 5th Avenue in Harlem, NY'. The key word here was 'house', as the event kicked off a new underground scene that would exist for decades to come.

The House of LaBeija was the first house in the ball scene. Houses are chosen families, usually made up of queer or trans youth who were homeless or rejected by their families. At the head is a house mother, who protects and provides for her children. Houses would often live together, eat together and compete together in balls.

These balls bore no resemblance to the pageantry and performance of the mostly white drag balls. They were elaborate competitions where contestants from different houses would walk in different categories: Realness, where trans women would compete to 'pass' as cisgender women; Runway, where participants would walk the catwalk emulating supermodels on fashion runways; and Face, where participants were required to seduce the judges by showing off their face like a beauty advert.

Then, there was Vogue.

Voguing is a style of movement and performance that was all about emulating the fierce angles of models in a certain fashion magazine. At first, voguing was performed to disco music, but house music soon took over as the soundtrack of choice. Voguing allowed queer and trans people of colour, who could never have imagined themselves in the glossy pages of *Vogue* magazine, to become celebrities among their own communities.

Soon, the angular poses that were crucial to voguing became known as the Old Way. In the 1980s, the New Way emerged, bringing with it the 'duck walk', as well as more hand expressions and acrobatics. This style was pioneered by the legend Willi Ninja, who helped bring vogue out of the underground.

Willi Ninja

Willi Ninja was born William Leake in Long Island, New York, in 1961. After finishing school he, like so many other young queer folk, packed up his things and headed for Greenwich Village. But, unlike many other queer folk, Willi was accepted and loved for who he was by his mother, who even supported his love of dance.

In the later 1970s, Willi joined the queer scene that congregated around the Christopher Street Piers, dancing early forms of vogue. He taught himself to dance and drew on an expansive list of inspirations, from Asian culture and martial arts (hence the name 'Ninja') to hieroglyphics, gymnastics and the work of classic American dancers like Fred Astaire and Michael Jackson. He added these influences into his voguing, shaping the dance form into something fierce, fast and expressive. Willi Ninja's martial arts influence meant the Vogue New Way was perfect for battling rival houses at the balls and settling disputes through dance.

Willi Ninja joined the ball community young, and as he grew to be a respected dancer in the scene, he took in and looked after new arrivals. Despite never having been a member of a 'house' himself, which would be typical for a house mother, Willi founded the House of Ninja in 1982. They were formidable at balls and known for their dancing prowess.

In 1991 Willi Ninja graced the screen in Jennie Livingston's cult classic documentary *Paris Is Burning* and was hailed as an electrifying new talent, not just as a dancer and choreographer but also as a runway model and fashion icon. He went on to walk for fashion houses like Chanel, Thierry Mugler and Jean Paul Gaultier, and even trained supermodels like Naomi Campbell in the art of grace and poise.

Willi Ninja used movement to defy gender conventions, shaping a dance form that continues to attract new generations of queer and trans people. Today, the House of Ninja still has chapters all around the globe, realising Willi's wishes of bringing ballroom to the world.

By 1990, vogue was everywhere, thanks to Madonna, whose 1989 song of the same name was topping charts around the world, with two members of the House of Xtravaganza choreographing and starring in the music video. Vogue classes were held at dance studios everywhere, and for the first time the creativity of the Black and Latiné LGBTQ+ community was valued.

However, in the eyes of the mainstream, voguing was all Madge. As with so much cultural appropriation, the trend moved on and took the spotlight away from the ball community. But uptown in Harlem, the ball culture continued to live on and in the mid 1990s evolved into a new New Way, called Vogue Femme.

Vogue culture contributed so much to modern queer culture, from music to dance and even language. Words and phrases often associated with queer culture like 'realness', 'fierce', 'yass queen', 'throwing shade' and 'slay' all descend from ball culture and, in particular, Black and Latiné transfeminine people. The houses behind this community were visionary in their creativity and style, and popular culture owes them so much. But while mainstream culture may have valued their *work*, when it came to their lives there was silence.

CHAPTER ELEVEN

Silence = Death

Most people find medical journals difficult to read, but for those able to wade through the dense scientific language, they're full of curiosities.

In June 1981, one particular medical journal noted a peculiar cluster of five young men in California who'd been diagnosed with rapid onset pneumocystis carinii pneumonia (PCP) – an extremely rare form of pneumonia that had previously only been observed in severely immunocompromised people. These young men had a history of otherwise good health. Two of them had already died. These cases were bewildering. The only commonality among the men was that they were homosexual.

Four weeks later, *The New York Times* published a news story under the headline, 'RARE CANCER SEEN IN 41 HOMOSEXUALS'. The cases were mostly centred around New York City and the San Francisco Bay Area, most of the men were under forty years old, and eight of them had died within two years of diagnosis. This rare cancer was called Kaposi's sarcoma. It initially appears as dark spots or lesions on the skin, then spreads to the lymph nodes and on to other parts of the body.

PCP and Kaposi's sarcoma were exceedingly rare conditions, and the fact that they were manifesting in gay men made the situation all the more baffling. Was it somehow related to amyl nitrate, or 'poppers', which gay men were partial to sniffing? No-one knew, so scientists started with what they did know (or at least, what they thought they knew): that it only affected homosexual men. As a result, by the end of 1981 this illness had been named 'gay-related immunodeficiency', or GRID. Doctors claim they didn't mean any disrespect to the gay community, but there is something deeply othering about naming a disease so generally after the group it targets. Then again, we're talking about the same medical culture that came up with 'female hysteria'. The name didn't last long, but it had a devastating impact on society. Like we said, medical terminology isn't for everyone, so among the general population the illness quickly became known as 'the gay plague'.

By 1983, the disease had spread around the Western world. The mysterious condition continued to mystify scientists, who did eventually discover that it wasn't just gay men who were falling ill – the disease also affected haemophiliacs, sex workers, blood recipients and injecting drug users. It also began to appear in the female partners of bisexual men who'd become ill, suggesting that it could be sexually transmitted. These new developments were enough to update the name to 'acquired immunodeficiency syndrome' or, as it's now more commonly known, AIDS.

By this stage, scientists knew they were on the precipice of an epidemic, but still thought they were monitoring an emerging disease.

They had no idea of the terror that was coming.

And it turned out, it had been waiting in the wings for a long time. Historical cases of AIDS have since been diagnosed that long pre-date the disease's 'discovery'. During the 1970s, injecting drug users, sex workers and poor communities knew there was something sinister around. Their friends were getting sick, but they didn't have health insurance and wouldn't have had the means nor the trust in the medical system to have their illness investigated. They mostly died at home, or on the street.

So scientists now had a name for the disease, but they still didn't know what caused it. It presented with all manner of symptoms. They knew it was spreading, which meant it was likely caused by a virus, but they couldn't identify the virus or work out where it had come from.

The answer may lie in colonisation. Ah yes, there it is again.

The current theory is that the virus that causes AIDS, like many viruses, originated in animals. In the Congo region of Africa, chimpanzees would become infected with a virus called SIV, or simian immunodeficiency virus, and when they were hunted by humans it would cross the species barrier. This happened many times, as far back as the 1880s, but it wasn't until the 1920s that the strain that would go on to cause AIDS would make the jump and begin to spread through the Congo, which at that time was under Belgian occupation. When the Belgian reign ended, an influx of Haitian people went to work in the Congo, where they were exposed to the virus, became infected and took it back to Haiti, from where it would spread to the United States.

Although it's widely accepted, the evidence of this origin story isn't rock solid. What we do know is that this theory led to another marginalised population being forced to wear the stigma of this disease. In fact, it led to the idea that Haitians, by nature of their race, were at high risk of contracting this illness.

An idea known as the 'four H's' soon began to circulate, which said that homosexuals, haemophiliacs, heroin addicts and Haitians were at the highest risk of contracting the virus, which in 1986 was finally named the human immunodeficiency virus, or HIV. Three of those four H's were then banned from donating blood. (Guess which ones.)

There are many parallels between the AIDS crisis and the COVID-19 pandemic, but for now we'll just note that COVID-19 introduced the world to an area of expertise few people knew existed (or how to pronounce): epidemiology. So let's run through a quick epidemiology lesson before we move on.

HIV is a virus that attacks CD4 cells, or T cells, which are a vital part of the body's immune system. When these cells fall below a certain level, HIV progresses to AIDS. This can take a number of years, but by the time it does happen, the body's immune system is so damaged it can't fight infections, meaning that even the most benign infection can become fatal. In the 1980s and early 90s, HIV/AIDS was a death sentence.

Young, vibrant, healthy people become entirely emaciated. Diarrhoea flowed uncontrollably from their frail bodies. Kaposi's sarcoma lesions would take over their hands, legs, arms and face. Certain infections would cause blindness, or nerve pain so unbearable it made walking impossible. People watched their friends and lovers go through the torture of trying to eat or drink with constant thrush in their mouth and oesophagus. They watched them drown from the fluid in their lungs. And then there was the dementia. When HIV spreads to the brain, patients lose their memory and their ability to concentrate and control their bodily functions. They become confused and no longer know what's happening or who is sitting beside their bed – if there's anyone at all.

Because that was the other pain that AIDS inflicted. People were terrified – of course they were. No-one knew how AIDS was spreading. They knew it could be sexually transmitted, but how were haemophiliacs becoming infected? Bodily fluids were the likely culprit, but which fluids? When? How?

Nobody was taking any chances. Patients suffered alone in hospital rooms, their meals left outside the door by medical staff who didn't want to risk being near them. Some doctors flat-out refused to treat people with AIDS. There was a genuine fear among the sick that they would be sent to die in internment camps, like the leper colonies of the past. People with AIDS were abandoned by the medical system, by the United States government (Ronald Reagan didn't even publicly acknowledge AIDS until 1987), often by their families and by a society that told themselves AIDS came for those who deserved it.

Not many people have the bravery required to stand in the face of this kind of fear and stigma. Then again, lesbians aren't just anyone.

THE STORY OF
The Blood Sisters of HIV/AIDS

In the years before AIDS, gay men often used lesbians as the butt of their sexist jokes, but in the early 1980s, this began to change. Lesbians watched on helplessly as the men in their community suffered, and while some argued against putting their own fight on hold to help the men, most came together, determined to find a way.

Lesbians took on the role of carers for men with AIDS, helping with shopping and daily tasks. They volunteered around the clock at hospitals, where they'd sit with the dying, talking to them and holding their hands. They became activists, taking part in demonstrations and heading up committees. They raised awareness and begged the men in their lives to use condoms. When a lack of men threatened the gay liberation movement, lesbians took on that work, too. They gave their time, their love, their skills and even their blood.

With gay men (as well as drug users and Haitians) banned from donating blood, there was a shortage of available blood for the regular transfusions needed by people with AIDS. In response, one group of lesbians in San Diego organised a lesbian blood drive. They expected a small group would roll up their sleeves, but over two hundred women turned up. They called themselves the Blood Sisters. Inspired, lesbians in other places began to organise their own blood drives too. Posters around cities read 'Our Boys Need Our Blood', and lesbians continued to donate, forming a reservoir of blood that went straight to those suffering.

The lesbian blood that pumped through the veins of these dying men was a living reminder that they were loved and not alone. People were fighting for them. And when the world turned a blind eye to their pain, this act provided the solidarity and kindness these men needed more than anything.

If you are lucky enough to have access to a queer archive, you might find flyers and other paraphernalia sporting an earlier version of our community's acronym. It always used to be 'GLBT', but in the years after the HIV/AIDS epidemic, the first two letters were switched, making the acronym 'LGBT'. This was a way of paying lesbians long overdue respect and acknowledging their sacrifices for a community in crisis.

As hospitals filled up with AIDS patients, the wait time for admission stretched to more than a month. The sick were dying on gurneys parked in the halls. But the public carried on like nothing was happening.

During the COVID-19 pandemic we saw many similarities. Many people ignored what was happening and carried on as usual. When discussing the death rate, contrarians pointed out that more deaths were caused by road accidents, or the flu, or smoking. The not-my-problem types said, 'It's only a big deal for people who are sick, old or disabled' – as though those lives are worth less. Some insisted the whole thing was a hoax.

While most of the world was convinced it was encountering these responses for the first time in their lifetime, there was a whole community of older queer and trans people who were experiencing the worst possible deja vu. The main difference was that COVID-19 commandeered the front pages, while AIDS for the most part remained a deadly footnote, an inconvenient story about a disease affecting those it was convenient to forget.

KNOW YOUR ICONS
Larry Kramer

Larry Kramer was a playwright, screenwriter and novelist who shook the gay scene with his controversial and candid novel *Faggots*, which chronicled gay life before AIDS. As he began to lose his community to AIDS, he co-founded the Gay Men's Health Crisis to offer support. But as the death toll among his personal circle reached twenty, Kramer wanted to do more than care for the sick – he wanted the government to do something. He wanted a cure.

In 1983, Kramer wrote an article in the *New York Native* titled '1,112 and Counting'. It begins, 'If this article doesn't scare the shit out of you, we're in real trouble. If this article doesn't rouse you to anger, fury, rage, and action, gay men may have no future on this earth. Our continued existence depends on just how angry you can get.'

The article was a call to action, written to shake gay men out of complacency and calling for the kind of direct-action tactics that had been used in the first years of gay liberation.

Over the next few years, as more of his friends became sick and died, Kramer spoke publicly and angrily about the Reagan administration's inaction and lack of funding towards AIDS research.

In 1987 he rallied three hundred activists to come together and founded a grassroots activist group called the AIDS Coalition to Unleash Power, or ACT UP. This group was one of the most successful activist groups in modern history, and was integral in making HIV/AIDS a treatable condition.

Just a week before the monumental formation of ACT UP, people with AIDS saw their first flicker of hope on the horizon: an abandoned cancer drug called AZT had been approved by the American Food and Drug Administration for the treatment of HIV/AIDS.

In a lab setting, AZT seemed to slow the virus, but in humans it was a costly trade-off. AZT is highly toxic, especially the dose that was approved by the FDA. It caused constant nausea, headaches and anaemia, but when the alternative was a painful death, these were side effects most people with AIDS were willing to weather.

It was also prohibitively expensive for most people – the drug was patented and the price set at $10,000 per year, which in the 1980s was way out of reach for most people. And then soon after, it became apparent that the virus continued to spread in people taking AZT. This exorbitant drug wasn't working. It might have been killing people faster.

ACT UP was furious at the focus on endless, slow clinical trials that resulted in worthless poisons that ruined what remained of the lives of sufferers. Larry Kramer wrote an open letter to Dr Anthony Fauci, then the director of the infectious disease centre at the National Institute of Health (NIH). He called Fauci a murderer, a pill-pushing pimp and a bastard.

You wouldn't think these kinds of accusations would warm Fauci to Kramer, but over the years the two became friends. They needed each other. Fauci didn't control the budgets going into AIDS research, so he needed the public anger of Kramer and ACT UP to push the NIH and the Reagan government for more money. And Kramer needed Fauci, too – he was one of few people in the NIH who actually listened to the activists and made things happen. Kramer knew the importance of having friends in high places.

177

ACT UP's 'Storm the NIH' protest on 21 May 1990: activists stage a die-in to demand the NIH expedite and broaden its research beyond AZT trials and into the AIDS-related diseases affecting women and people of colour.

ACT UP soon became a sprawling organisation with many international affiliates that covered different aspects of the fight against AIDS, from awareness and education to treatment and research. They became experts in the condition, learning to read medical studies and decipher the results so they could hold medical experts to account.

When these results weren't made public, they zapped. ACT UP was responsible for brilliant, provocative zaps like die-ins, where activists would hold up traffic by playing dead in the road, lying limp as the police dragged them away. They would protest outside the NIH by creating a fake graveyard, each tombstone calling for action. They chained themselves to the New York Stock Exchange to protest the price of AZT, and in one notorious zap, they covered a senator's house in a giant condom. In London, they threw condoms over the walls of prisons, protesting the fact that prisoners weren't allowed them. In France, they stormed their way into offices of pharmaceutical companies, smearing fake blood along the walls and drenching early computers.

For the members of ACT UP, days were for rage and nights were for raves. After demonstrating in the day, activists would come together to dance to house and electronica. These raves were a quasar of compassion and kindness. DJs would tell every person in the room with HIV or AIDS to put their hands up. Hands would rise around the room and the crowd would roar with love. There was unimaginable pain, but profound beauty, too.

The political approach of ACT UP, while era defining, wasn't the only way the community tackled the crisis. Another group active against AIDS focussed on educating gay men around safe-sex practices, and they did so entirely in drag.

Sisters of Perpetual Indulgence

The Sisters of Perpetual Indulgence are an order of queer nuns that formed in San Francisco just before the onset of the AIDS crisis. They set out to use camp as a political tool, appropriating traditional Catholic symbols to parody the archaic moral attitudes of the Catholic Church, raise awareness of the issues the LGBTQ+ community faced in the Castro – San Francisco's gaybourhood – and make a loud, visible statement about gender and sexuality.

The Sisters of Perpetual Indulgence mixed visible masculinity with strictly feminine religious elements like nun's habits, and added shock value by wearing clown-like drag make-up and punk accessories. The overall look was reminiscent of a schlocky Halloween film that parodied society's fear of homosexuals. They gave themselves names like Sister Roz Erection, Sister Florence Nightmare and Sister Missionary Position. As the order expanded around the world, some chapters grew to involve lesbian monks known as 'Brothers' as well.

As you might imagine, the Sisters of Perpetual Indulgence didn't need to do much to grab attention – just the look of them inspired outrage from conservatives, and curious giggles from everyone else. But the order wasn't a drag performance for entertainment; it was what some scholars have called 'serious parody' – and their silliness carried a deadly serious message.

When AIDS arrived at the Castro, the Sisters of Perpetual Indulgence began challenging the church's moralising and educating the community about the disease. Even today quality, accessible sex education feels like a big ask, but in the early 1980s the situation was dire. The Sisters produced plain-language safe-sex guides that taught men how to keep themselves and their partners safe from the transmission of HIV. A group of genderfucking nuns preaching the importance of safe sex is already pretty powerful, but the order went further, delivering ceremonies, exorcisms and other religious rites to tackle homophobia, transphobia and stigma in the community.

Somewhat surprisingly, many Sisters were actually of Christian faith. On the whole, they weren't anti-religion (though some Sisters were). They believed that queerness was spiritual, and that whatever cosmic forces existed, queer and transgender people were a divine part of that.

As the number of AIDS-related deaths rose, the Sisters' role evolved to become distinctly, well, nun-like. The order filled a void in the community that the church might have in a less homophobic world. To be told that you were HIV positive was the most devastating blow imaginable, bringing guilt, shame, regret, sadness, anger and above all fear of what was to come. Suicides were common, as men did not want to live through the pain of dying. In these situations, the Sisters provided something like pastoral care and a point of spiritual connection. They brought people together, comforted the grieving and sat with the dying. They added meaning to what remained of people's short lives, and that makes the Sisters of Perpetual Indulgence closer to the divine than any institution they parodied.

The AIDS crisis birthed some of the most impactful imagery of the twentieth century – an order of nuns in punk drag is just one example. The crisis was concentrated on gay men and those who used drugs, which meant the crisis was concentrated on the creative scene. The fashion, design and advertising industries were all hit particularly hard, as was the art scene, so people from these spaces were the most active allies.

The fashion industry rallied together during the AIDS crisis in support of the many lives lost. Prominent fashion figures like Donna Karan, Michael Kors, Marc Jacobs and stylist Patricia Field (who would go on to create Carrie Bradshaw's iconic wardrobe in *Sex and the City*) hosted massive fashion sales and charity vogue balls and auctioned off exclusive pieces, with all funds going towards the sick.

While Madonna profited greatly off the creativity of ball culture, she was also one of the community's most active allies at this time, raising millions of dollars for research and treatment, as well as smuggling experimental drugs from Mexico into the US in an attempt to help people she knew. When her close friend Keith Haring passed away from AIDS, Madonna declared the final leg of her Blond Ambition Tour a benefit concert, with all ticket sales going to AIDS research.

Keith Haring

The work of Keith Haring is some of the most widely recognised and accessible in the world. His simple line drawings, bursting with playful energy, are naive in form but complex in message.

Haring grew up in the 1960s in love with cartoons. He drew his way through school and enrolled in a commercial art course in Pittsburgh, but soon realised he had little interest in becoming a commercial artist. He dropped out and wound up at New York's School of Visual Arts. At the time, New York City was the epicentre of the alt art world. Keith soon fell into this scene, and met his good friend and another iconic artist, Jean-Michel Basquiat.

At the time, graffiti as a genuine art form was still in its infancy, but Haring was drawn to the idea of placing artworks in public spaces. He found unused advertising spaces in the New York subway and turned them into a canvases for his artistic experimentation. He'd refer to the subway as his 'laboratory', an open studio where he could play with new ideas. On one prolific day, Haring completed forty pieces of subway art. Commuters found his art charming, and enjoyed seeing new pieces on their route.

As Haring's following grew, he began to do group shows with other artists, and eventually opened his famous 'Pop Shop', which was a retail space selling T-shirts, badges and other merchandise emblazoned with his art. Despite having dropped out of a commercial art course, Keith Haring was a pioneer in exploring the intersection between art and commerce. The art world at the time was disgusted at the idea of what they thought was dumbing down art for the masses, but Keith saw this as a way of bringing the masses into the art world. Commerce for Keith was about accessibility, which is why his artwork continues to appear on everything from watches and hoodies to socks and mugs. Selling out was the whole point.

Haring's belief that art needed to be available to all also drove him to create public murals everywhere from Pisa to Melbourne, and frequently these public works would have a strong social message.

Haring became fascinated with semiotics and how we attach meaning to different symbols. He'd use slogans like 'Crack Is Whack' to raise awareness about crack cocaine, and shapes like mushroom clouds to protest nuclear war. And throughout the 1980s, he would create icon-rich artworks to protest the US government's inaction around AIDS, greatly contributing to the rich visual language of the fight against this disease.

In 1988, after years of using his art to call for action on AIDS, Keith Haring received his own HIV diagnosis. He continued his work fervently until he became too sick. Haring passed away from AIDS-related complications at the age of just thirty-one. The year before he died, he established the Keith Haring Foundation to provide funding and imagery to AIDS organisations and children's programs.

183

SILENCE = DEATH

SILENCE=DEATH

Art and activism have always been close friends, but ACT UP really knew how to design a movement.

Perhaps the most striking visual of the crisis was ACT UP's own, for want of a better word, branding. It used one of the most subversive symbols of the era, the pink triangle, drawing a powerful connection between the murders committed by the Nazis and the murder of queer and trans people through government inaction on AIDS. With just two words and a symbol, ACT UP managed to encapsulate their entire mission. Ask anyone in advertising and they'll tell you that's no easy feat.

As the 1990s rolled around, some places had achieved relative success in bringing new HIV infections down, through a combination of community education and government fearmongering.

In the UK, terrifying advertisements with falling tombstones told Britons not to 'die of ignorance', creating a climate of fear around sex so intense it stopped people going to bathhouses, bars and clubs. While this helped to stem new infections, it placed even more blame and stigma on the sick.

So too did an advertisement featuring a grim reaper in a bowling alley knocking down innocent families, which became a fixture in Australian living rooms.

But as the rate of new infections fell, the death toll from those already living with HIV/AIDS continued to rise – at a devastating rate.

In New York, wearied by weekly funerals and dwindling participation numbers, tensions began to rise in the ACT UP mothership. Initially, AIDS didn't discriminate – men who had sex with men were given the same fatal diagnosis regardless of their position in society. However, as the crisis wore on, certain privileges began to affect the movement. The reality was that middle-class gay and bisexual men had far more access to decision makers than other groups affected by HIV/AIDS. They were more likely to have jobs in medical institutions or know people who did, and they could use these connections to create real change inside the companies. This access was vital, and the men within ACT UP exploited it well.

But there were many, many female victims who had no such access and faced additional issues that weren't being addressed. For starters, the way AIDS manifested in female bodies was different. As research wasn't being conducted on female bodies, the AIDS-related conditions affecting them weren't often covered under insurance definitions of AIDS. They had to fight for abortion rights, for their bodies to be involved in clinical trials, and to be listened to by doctors.

People of colour were also left out of research and clinical trials, so couldn't be sure how treatments would affect their bodies. Historically, when people of colour had taken part in medical research, the placebo was often given to Black participants. People of colour worried that even if they were able to access trials, they would again be given the placebo, their fate effectively sealed.

Just as they had in the Gay Liberation Front years earlier, these issues caused a split. In 1992, those who had boardroom access branched off to focus on research and treatment, leaving the remaining factions within the movement hanging in the balance.

The remaining activists continued their direct-action tactics, and by now they were more desperate, more angry than ever. The lives of those lost to AIDS complications continued to be celebrated in beautiful memorials, including a breathtaking AIDS memorial quilt with each square dedicated to a person who died with the virus. Magnificent as these tributes were, some activists felt like they were obscuring the ugly, devastating reality that was taking place.

So ACT UP New York, working with their Washington counterparts, organised their most powerful protest yet.

On Sunday 11 October 1992 at 1 pm, ACT UP activists marched towards the White House with signs calling for the Bush administration to act. They carried small boxes, and as they reached the gates of the White House, they began throwing the contents of these boxes onto the lawn. The ashes of their loved ones, their friends, their fellow activists, their lovers, their sons, brothers, sisters and others rained down on the White House, covering its entrance in the dust of the dead.

Many activists living with AIDS called for their remains or their dying bodies to be used politically. These actions were known as political funerals, and they occurred in many places all over the world.

In later years, they became less necessary thanks to medical breakthroughs that would be transformative for people living with HIV. By the mid 90s, a cocktail of drugs was discovered that was able to suppress the HIV virus and stop it from progressing to AIDS. Over the decade, this combination of drugs proved to be able to keep the levels of the virus so low it was undetectable and untransmittable, meaning people with HIV could live as long as those without it. A decade later, an even more revolutionary development would emerge – a daily drug that would prevent someone from becoming infected.

With these life-altering developments, HIV/AIDS has faded from the cultural conversation. But that doesn't mean it's no longer an issue. According to UNAIDS, the United Nations program dedicated to eradicating HIV, in 2020 there were approximately 37.7 million people living with HIV. Every year people of all ages continue to contract the virus. Although very effective, current treatments remain prohibitively costly. Some of the drugs are still gatekept behind patents that mean lower-income countries can't access them. In 2020, 9.8 million people were living with untreated HIV, and approximately 680,000 died from AIDS-related complications. The battle against this virus is far from over, and it's not being spoken about. Silence equals death, and there is still too much of both.

CHAPTER TWELVE

The Internet Is the New Gay Bar

In 1990 at New York Pride, by then entering its third decade, a zine was distributed among the crowd titled *Queers Read This!* The cover proclaimed it was 'Published anonymously by Queers', and the zine created waves simply through its reclamation of the word 'queer', which was still considered an offensive slur at the time.

The anonymous queers behind the zine were part of a new organisation called Queer Nation, which was formed by activists from ACT UP in response to a spike in hate crimes against queer and trans people. If you've ever heard the chant 'We're here, we're queer, get used to it!' – that's them.

Queers Read This! was a call for queer people across all identities to get angry about the murders and bashings occurring in a community that was still being decimated by AIDS. The writing drips with love and rage. There are lines like 'You as an alive and functioning queer are a revolutionary' and, in an echo of an ancient idea, 'An army of lovers cannot lose'. It's a rousing read, and it was effective – not just in reclaiming 'queer' as a uniting term, but also as a piece of alternative media.

In the 1990s and early 2000s, the media had a very complicated relationship with LGBTQ+ people. The AIDS epidemic had led to increased stigma of gay and bisexual men, as well as trans women, and soon newspaper headlines would report a sharp rise in gay bashings and brutal murders. Between the news stories we had Madonna and George Michael queering the screen with their music videos. Over the next decade, new media would shape LGBTQ+ people more than any other force, and the results were good, bad and downright ugly.

From the mid 1980s, greater access to photocopiers and print technology meant that zines and independent magazines proliferated as a way for LGBTQ+ people to share information and ideas. Grassroots community groups would publish independent magazines as guides to help queer and trans people connect with each other and their identities.

One of these was published by the Bay Area Bisexual Network, titled *Anything that Moves* – a reclamation of the popular misconception that bisexual people are attracted to anything that moves. In 1991, *Anything that Moves* published something that would shape bisexual politics for decades: *The Bisexual Manifesto.*

The manifesto explained that while progress had been made in the lives of gay and lesbian people, there had been no such progress specific to the bi experience. It combated ideas that bisexuals were confused, unsatisfied with relationships, and that they adopted a binary view of gender, pointing out that bisexuality meant attraction to *more than one* gender. Somehow, society is *still* struggling with that idea. Bisexual people were largely ignored or invalidated by the mainstream gay and lesbian movement, which led to more outspoken bisexual activists, like Brenda Howard.

Brenda Howard

Brenda Howard was a Jewish bisexual rights activist, sex-positive feminist and polyamorist who was instrumental in lobbying for 'bisexual' to be added to the title of the 1993 Gay and Lesbian March in Washington, and more broadly for a 'B' to be included after 'G' and 'L' to form what would become the LGBTQ+ acronym.

But Howard's bisexual activism began long before the 1990s. She was on the organising committee of the first ever Christopher Street Liberation Day march, having known many of the people who were inside Stonewall on the night of the uprising. Howard helped popularise the term 'pride' to counter the shame society placed on her community, and that the community sadly placed upon themselves. She used the word 'pride' to describe her bisexuality, which at the time was an invisible identity that was subject to all the hate gay and lesbian identities were, as well as stigma from the gay and lesbian community themselves, who felt that bisexuals betrayed the movement by pursuing heterosexual relationships.

Howard was steadfast in advocating the idea that bisexual people were neither confused nor greedy, but rather entirely certain of themselves. She had a badge that read: 'Bi, Poly, Switch. I Know What I Want.' Her politics were distinctly radical and queer, intertwining her bisexual activism with her sex-positive feminism, which included polyamory as well as kink, and anything that stood against the heterosexist hegemony that governed society.

But Howard's serious activism was complemented by an excellent sense of humour. Once, having been arrested and locked up in jail, Howard read aloud from steamy novels until the police, highly uncomfortable, agreed to release her and the other activists on the spot.

She dedicated her life to fostering the bisexual community, even setting up a phone hotline that bisexual New Yorkers could call to learn about upcoming bi events, and establishing the first Alcoholics Anonymous chapter for bisexuals. These grassroots initiatives built up the bi identity as an entirely legitimate sexuality on its own, with politics and struggles separate to those of the gay and lesbian communities.

Throughout the later part of her life, Howard championed a 'Still Bisexual' campaign that targeted the bi-erasure of those in different-sex relationships. She passed away from colon cancer in 2005, during Pride – on the thirty-fifth anniversary of the event she helped create. Her partner in the final years of her life, Larry Nelson, created a video after her death in which he holds up a sign that reads #StillBisexual and says, 'Beside the fact that we were together and I am straight, I know if she was alive, she would be here holding a sign saying "I'm #StillBisexual". Since she is not with us anymore, I will hold one up for her.'

While the underground media was disseminating a distinctly inclusive and progressive take on bisexuality, the mainstream media were ever so slightly missing the mark. Make no mistake, the 1990s was a brilliant period for LGBTQ+ representation compared to previous decades (and as they say, don't let the perfect be the enemy of the good). But while glossy magazines enthusiastically reported a rise in bisexuality, they did so with none of the nuance or understanding present in *The Bisexual Manifesto*.

In 1995, *Newsweek* ran a cover that read: 'Bisexuality. Not Gay. Not Straight. A new sexual identity emerges.' Other news articles from the period seem almost self-congratulatory in their reporting of the culture's brand new 'anything goes' sexuality, pointing to Madonna as a role model who makes it okay to go *both* ways. Words like 'bi-curious' and 'heteroflexible' were used to describe ostensibly heterosexual women going gay for the day. The downside to what appeared to be a celebration of progressive sexuality was the insinuation that bisexuality was flippant, more of a hobby than a genuine, complex and nuanced identity.

The 1990s were the pinnacle of women's fashion magazines; *Cosmopolitan*, *Vogue*, *Cleo* and *Vanity Fair* set women's tastes around the world. Around the time this 'new sexual identity' (*Newsweek*'s words, not ours) emerged, fashion magazines were taking a group previously ridiculed as the pariahs of style and repackaging them as the height of fashion. The trend was named 'lesbian chic', and it took androgynous suits, biker jackets and undercut hair and made them high fashion.

It's not like lesbians weren't fashionable before – some of the fashion industry's most influential talents have been lesbians, and the 1920s were of course a high point of sapphic style. It's more that for the previous seventy-odd years, lesbians had enjoyed the fact that their style was out of fashion, using their haircuts, boots and blazers to identify one another. But then *Vanity Fair* released the now-iconic photoshoot featuring supermodel Cindy Crawford pretending to shave butch musician KD Lang's jawline. Lesbian style was back.

But while underground zines and fashion magazines were walking (okay, stumbling) in step towards more widespread acceptance for queer people, there was another group who continued to be outcast from society: transgender people.

In the early 1990s, the word 'transgender' still wasn't widely used, but it was gaining traction. Prior to this, there was awareness around 'transvestites', who were assigned male at birth, presented as women but had not medically transitioned, and 'transsexuals', who had had medically transitioned in what was colloquially known as a 'sex change'.

As the use of the term 'transgender' increased, the terms 'transvestite' and 'transexual' began to blend under the idea that transgender people identify with a gender other than the one they were assigned at birth, and that some choose to affirm that gender through their gender expression or through hormone treatment and surgery.

The power of language cannot be understated – what the word 'transgender' offered was the idea of gender as being entirely separate to sex. This one word managed to shape an entire consciousness around a concept that had existed since the beginning of time. More than that, the word became a unifying identity that spanned a multitude of experiences, possibilities and politics.

In 1992 an anti-racist white, working-class, secular Jewish, transgender, lesbian, female, revolutionary communist named Leslie Feinberg published hir (yes, hir – we'll get to that) own zine, titled *Transgender Liberation*. In this zine, Feinberg framed the word 'transgender' as an umbrella term, encapsulating the kaleidoscope of experiences of transsexuals, cross-dressers, drag queens, so-called transvestites, butch lesbians and all people whose gender expression is at odds with the sex they were assigned at birth.

In *Transgender Liberation*, much as we have tried to do in this book, Feinberg traces the transgender experience back to its pre-colonial roots, determining that transgender people have always existed – it is, in fact, 'passing' that is new. The assumption that transgender people strive to be perceived by complete strangers as their correct gender is relatively recent. Prior to colonisation, trans people did not need to adhere to cisgender norms to validate their gender identity. They were just them.

KNOW YOUR ICONS
Leslie Feinberg

Leslie Feinberg was a pioneer in opening up the multitude of possibilities the transgender experience and identity has to offer. As you read hir story, you'll notice different pronouns – these aren't typos, but a set of neo-pronouns Feinberg used to resist assumptions around gender and sexuality.

Feinberg was born in 1949 and spent most of hir youth in Buffalo, New York. Hir family did not accept hir gender nonconformity, so Feinberg supported hirself working odd jobs in factories and once in a book bindery. For people like Feinberg – a dyke, a butch, a transmasculine person – life in Buffalo wasn't kind. Work was hard to come by, discrimination was insurmountable and 'corrective rape' a reality.

Leslie Feinberg wrote about life as a working-class butch in hir debut novel, *Stone Butch Blues*. While not technically an autobiography, the novel offers a window into a life that had rarely been deemed worthy of interest. Few novels have tapped into a collective queer consciousness in the way *Stone Butch Blues* does. Many people resonate with the story of a working-class masculine yet non-male person growing up isolated, experiencing the pain of the body's betrayal during puberty and trying to navigate the delicate interplay of gender and sexuality. Transmasculine and butch people are among the most marginalised, and for them *Stone Butch Blues* has been a legitimately life-saving tonic.

As the transgender revolution gained momentum, the conflict between the transgender community and the wider gay and lesbian movement continued to escalate. As transgender people continued to be excluded from events that named lesbian, gay and (eventually, after much crusading) bisexual people in their titles, Feinberg, along with transgender activist Riki Wilchins, founded an activist organisation called the Transexual Menace. The Transexual Menace drew on the success of the Lavender Menace, which had protested lesbian exclusion from the women's movement; like the Lavender Menace, the Transexual Menace also had T-shirts, but theirs featured the group's name in *Rocky Horror Picture Show*–esque text dripping blood, to mock the movement's fear of transgender people.

The Transexual Menace continued to use irony to their advantage. When a lesbian feminist event, the Michigan Womyn's Music Festival, banned trans women from attending, arguing that trans women were not 'womyn-born womyn', Feinberg and Wilchins organised an annual protest called Camp Trans, which was held outside the festival. Despite these protests, the Michigan Womyn's Music Festival retained their anti-trans policy for years.

Leslie Feinberg and the Transexual Menace made great leaps in transgender visibility, drawing attention to the murders of transgender people and the lack of outrage from society and the police. There are echoes of *Stone Butch Blues* in the story of Brandon Teena, a transgender man from Nebraska who – just a few months after Feinberg's novel was released – was raped and murdered at the age of twenty-one. Teena's story galvanised the trans community and their allies in such a way that it became the subject of the film *Boys Don't Cry*. The Menace hosted vigils outside the courthouse during the sentencing of Teena's murderer, and also protested the media coverage of Teena, which described him as a confused, cross-dressing lesbian who presented male due to childhood trauma. Once again, the media were perpetuating tired stereotypes about trans people.

Feinberg continued to write to raise awareness around the breadth of transgender identities, following up hir 1992 zine with a book, *Transgender Warriors*, which traced the history of trans people.

Leslie Feinberg lived with Lyme disease and suffered a multitude of health problems, passing away in 2014 as a result of complications. Hir last words were 'Hasten the revolution! Remember me as a revolutionary communist' – and so we will, but ze will also be remembered as a pioneer who helped put into language what it means to be trans.

In the early days of the 1990s, zines provided a necessary antidote to the mainstream media's framing of queer and transgender people. Self-publishing for this purpose goes all the way back to Karl Heinrich Ulrichs' own 'zines', published in the nineteenth century. The emergence of a queercore punk scene popularised zine making as a way for marginalised queer and trans people to circulate subversive ideas. During the AIDS crisis, zines provided information about prevention and treatment. Community media was used for everything from education to news bulletins, event guides, travel advice, information sharing and even hook-up ads.

So when a new media emerged that offered these same possibilities with global access and no printing costs, it's no surprise that queer and transgender people used it early, and well.

By the mid 1990s, the World Wide Web was changing everything. For transgender people in the midst of a revolution, the internet was a newly accessible tool to exchange experiences and stories. Bulletin boards and forums were used to share photos and details of gender-affirming surgeries, as well as offer advice and information about practitioners. Activism blossomed online, allowing transgender groups to organise across borders and reach a broader audience. The advent of email and newsletters meant information could be shared in real time, and naturally the conversations occurring in digital spaces continued to shape the transgender consciousness.

Digital activists emerged, like transgender woman Gwendolyn Smith, who ran the Transgender Community Forum on AOL (one of the first transgender forums on the internet) from 1991 until 1998. Gwendolyn built on her digital activism to establish the Transgender Day of Remembrance, to memorialise and bring awareness to the overwhelming number of transgender people who die as a result of transphobia. Today, there's a digital companion called the Remembering Our Dead project, which plots the deaths of transgender people on an open-source map.

One other crucial part of the relationship between 'transness' and the internet is the idea of digital gender expression. Trans people had the opportunity to present as their true gender online and experiment with their expression – all without compromising their physical safety.

When the new millennium arrived, it brought another key development: gay and lesbian dating sites. By the year 2000, at least two dating sites exclusively for gay men existed in Gaydar and Manhunt, as well as Pink Sofa, a dating site exclusively for lesbian and bisexual women. This meant people could meet in relative secrecy, without having to risk exposure. It also meant that your new lover could be from any time zone. The uptake of that would become a lesbian in-joke over the next decade.

When OkCupid emerged a few years later, providing a free dating site that allowed for multiple sexualities and gender identities, queer dating became a favourite pastime. In the 2010s these sites became apps, and dating became something you could do at the bus stop.

With this development, one app would emerge to rule them all – Grindr. This one app is behind so much of gay male culture. It removed the need for gay bars as gateway to sex; it removed the fear of meeting someone for the first time; it removed the clothing of millions of men. It changed the game in numerous ways, some of which we're still figuring out.

Grindr wasn't the only invention that shaped queer and trans lives online. In 2007, Tumblr arrived to shake things up, bringing queer and trans culture to an entirely new generation. Tumblr provided trans people with something profound, a kind of digital body, in blog form. Transgender people, at whatever age and stage of their transition, suddenly had a blank page on which to build their identity from the ground up. They explored their gender in a way that could be edited as they discovered themselves. They tried out pronouns and ways of expressing their transness online, granting grammar more widespread cultural importance than ever before.

THE UNNECESSARILY COMPLICATED HISTORY OF
The Pronoun 'They'

If you went back in time and spoke to one of the figures in this book, we guarantee they would be baffled to hear that at one point, the fight for LGBTQ+ liberation hinged on one of the most benign and ubiquitous words in the English language: they.

As awareness around non-binary identities has risen and more people have identified with that label, using the pronouns 'they' and 'them' to describe oneself has become increasingly accepted. However, a not-insignificant group of people continue to fight against these pronouns, disguising their preference for binary genders as a profound respect of grammar (pretty sure only a minority of these people have ever shown any previous interest in grammar). So, let's have a short grammar lesson to clear a few things up.

Up until the 1880s, the singular 'they' was actually the main pronoun to describe an unnamed person. It was used not only by the public, but also by writers like Jane Austen and Shakespeare, who are a pretty big deal in the English language. But grammarists began to want English grammar to follow the more prestigious Latin, a language where all words have a gender. That left us with 'he' and 'she'.

People still wanted a generic singular pronoun to describe a person whose gender is unknown or irrelevant, which led to the adoption of 'he' as the default pronoun. You can imagine how this went down with feminists. From the suffragettes to the second wave of the 70s, feminists fought to destroy the generic 'he' – but even feminist academics didn't want to lose their scholarly Latin allegiance by resorting to 'they'. A string of other gender-neutral singular pronouns were suggested. These included ze/hir, as used by Leslie Feinberg, as well as xe and ve and other neo pronouns. These pronouns are still in use, but the singular 'they' is still the most popular alternative to 'he' and 'she'.

Languages adapt and change all the time – if they didn't, we'd still be speaking in ancient tongues and you'd be able to decipher Sappho's poetry yourself – but if there are any language traditionalists in your life, tell them not to worry, because the singular 'they' has been just fine for a long, long time.

Tumblr birthed a new era of queer and trans culture, with memes, fashion, music and flags. So many flags. The Rainbow Flag, created in 1978 by Gilbert Baker, underwent a period of rapid iteration. The horizontal stripes changed colours to become specific flags for a spectrum of other identities, including transgender, bisexual, lesbian, non-binary, asexual, pansexual, omnisexual, agender, aromantic, ally and a constantly evolving list of others.

While the Rainbow Flag accumulated spin-offs, it also evolved to become more actively inclusive of people of colour and transgender people and well as recognise those lost to the AIDS crisis. This new version, called the Progress Pride flag, was created by artist and designer Daniel Quasar in 2018 and continues to evolve to best represent our community.

The internet and then social media became crucial forums for people to discuss and discover their identities and find spaces of belonging. In countries whose laws and cultures are more accepting of queer and trans people, this process can be a joyous journey of self-exploration – and can result in a lot of memes. But in other countries, like those where laws criminalising homosexuality are still in place, social networks like TikTok and Twitter are crucial for LGBTQ+ people to be able to connect with each other safely. There are still over sixty-five countries where consensual same-sex activity is a crime, many with prison sentences between ten years and life, and at least six where the death penalty is implemented.

Do You Listen to Mashrou' Leila?

Recently (but not so recently that we're about to blow their cover), queer people in south-west Asian and North African countries would use their own version of 'Do you listen to Girl in Red?' – the coded phrase used by lesbians on TikTok – to identify themselves as queer to other queer people. They'd ask, 'Do you listen to Mashrou' Leila?'

Mashrou' Leila are a Lebanese indie band that formed in Beirut in 2008. They became wildly popular during the Arab Spring – a series of uprisings and rebellions in the Middle East and North Africa beginning in 2010 – and their lyrics, which tackle topics like politics and homosexuality, have led to government censorship and death threats from religious conservatives, some so severe that the band has been pulled from festival line-ups in the name of reducing bloodshed.

Hamed Sinno, the band's singer, is openly queer, which makes performing on stage dangerous in many of the countries the band tour in. Their relative popularity, along with their queer singer, made 'Do you listen to Mashrou' Leila?' a perfect code to use on heavily moderated social media – but when the consequences of being discovered are so high, especially in countries like Saudi Arabia and the United Arab Emirates, these codes must change constantly.

In 2017 Mashrou' Leila would move from being a code word among a covert community to a symbol in the fight for human rights. The band was playing a show in Cairo when, moved by the music and the crowd, a queer woman named Sarah Hegazi climbed atop her friend's shoulders and unfurled a rainbow flag. In a photo snapped by another friend in the moment (one that could honestly be an album cover), Hegazi is seen beaming.

But a week after the photo was taken, amid Egypt's zero-tolerance crackdown on LGBTQ+ people, Hegazi was arrested and held in prison for three months awaiting trial. She was brutally tortured, enduring extensive periods in solitary confinement, electric shocks, beatings and sexual assault. When she was finally released, Hegazi was diagnosed with severe PTSD. She sought asylum in Canada, where she joined a socialist group and continued advocating for human rights, but the trauma of her time in prison never abated. Continuing to suffer PTSD and severe depression, in 2020 Sarah Hegazi ended her own life. Her last words were of forgiveness for a world that took so much from her.

In the days after Sarah's death, Mashrou' Leila shared a statement in mourning of Sarah and all LGBTQ+ people living under the ever-present threat of persecution and violence. Despite increasing censorship, the band continues to advocate for LGBTQ+ rights, and their name has become less of a whispered code and more of a rallying cry.

Sarah Hegazi's death was a catalyst for a global movement. Stencils of her face against a rainbow flag began appearing on walls around the world. On Twitter #RaiseTheFlagForSarah trended globally, and the photo of Sarah wrapped in the rainbow flag proliferated endlessly on Instagram. Like a digital wind, algorithms swept the fury of our community further and faster than activists of the previous decade could ever have thought possible.

LGBTQ+ people have a complex relationship with the media – we've spent so much of history as both headlines and footnotes. But over the last few decades we have, through technology, been given agency, and more opportunities to tell our own stories. The impacts of social media on society won't be wholly understood for a long time, but as queer venues continue to decline, the internet is giving us spaces to connect, discuss, organise, hook up, and create our own culture. It allows us to document our lives and experiences so that, hopefully, in the future, when historians are writing about this point in time, they won't be relying on old court documents for scant details of queer life. Instead, they'll simply look up a hashtag and it will all be right there.

This photo of Sarah Hegazi went viral on social media after her death. In gaining permission to publish her image, we were asked to attribute it to 'Friends of Sarah who can't be named', a reminder that to live and love freely is a privilege and there is still much work to be done.

An Army of Lovers Cannot Lose

We should probably leave it there. Our community's history is unfolding right now, all around us, and we're going to need hindsight to be able to make sense of it. If the past five thousand years have taught us anything, it's that progress isn't linear. Queer and trans people have been accepted, celebrated, feared and loathed at different points in time. In Germany in the 1930s, we saw how quickly a trend towards acceptance could veer so far off course. We've seen how the most irrelevant details can drastically alter our lives – for centuries. One sixteenth-century English king wanting a divorce resulted in homosexuality being criminalised around the world, and in more than thirty-five countries (at the time of writing), that king's law remains in place. On the other hand, our community has responded brilliantly with new languages, art, philosophy, film, theatre, literature, jazz, disco, house music, drag, dance and fashion.

We can't be complacent; there is still so much work to be done. Transgender people, especially trans women of colour, continue to have their lives stolen and their deaths unreported. Our community is still criminalised and inhumanely punished in numerous places. Our elders, who fought for our rights at Stonewall or the first Mardi Gras, are now the first generation of openly queer and trans people navigating systemic discrimination in aged care. Between edits of this book, new bills have been introduced in different parts of the world designed to erode the rights and freedoms of our community. These bills often have benign-enough sounding names. Names like Paragraph 175. Or the Labouchere Amendment. We know not to let these names fool us.

While we focus on these issues, we also need to find joy in what the future holds. After all, every person who featured in this book has played some small (or large) part in contributing to the freedoms and culture we do have today. If they were still alive, there's a lot we'd love to show them.

It's also important to acknowledge that if many of the people mentioned in this book were alive today, we might not like them very much. History has smoothed the rougher edges of many of these people who, while revolutionary in some way, also came with their own prejudices and flaws born from the struggles of their era. If we can balance all this, we have the opportunity to connect with millions of members of our community across space and time.

The idea for *Rainbow History Class* came from the realisation that if we had the opportunity to learn about the lives of queer and trans people, we might come into ourselves sooner and perhaps be happier. Figuring yourself out can be isolating, especially if it seems like you're the only queer kid in town. By learning the stories of people just like us, people who've felt the feelings we have, we can feel less alone. We can imagine that behind us is an army of people who have fought, over centuries, so that we can live and love as we are. With an army of lovers behind us – as well as friends and fighters and artists and scientists and kings and queens and emperors and house mothers and rebels and film stars – we cannot lose.

Thank you for coming to class.

Further Reading

If you want to continue discovering queer and trans history, here are some sources we recommend. While only a selection of what we used in our research, these were all invaluable in shaping this book.

ARTICLES

'Gay Men Under the Nazi Regime', Holocaust Encyclopedia, United States Holocaust Memorial Museum

'Homosexuality', Brent Pickett, *The Stanford Encyclopedia of Philosophy*

'Lesbianism and the Criminal Law of England and Wales', Caroline Derry, OpenLearn

'Paragraph 175 and the Nazi Campaign against Homosexuality', Holocaust Encyclopedia, United States Holocaust Memorial Museum

Queers Read This! (zine) Published anonymously by Queers, 1990

'The 1619 Project', *The New York Times Magazine*

'The Changing Nature of Lubunca, Turkey's LGBTQ slang', Pesha Magid, Atlas Obscura

'The Erasure of Islam from the Poetry of Rumi', Rozina Ali, *The New Yorker*

'The Queen Who Would be King', Elizabeth B Wilson, *Smithsonian Magazine*

'The Trials of Oscar Wilde: An Account', Douglas O'Linder, Famous Trials

'Two Women Walk into a Theatre Bathroom: The Fanny and Stella Trials as Trans Narrative', Simon Joyce, *Victoria Review*

'We'wha', Mariana Brandman, National Women's History Museum

DOCUMENTARIES

How to Survive a Plague, David France (2012)

Kumu Hina, Dean Hamer and Joe Wilson (2014)

Paris Is Burning, Jennie Livingston (1991)

Pay It No Mind: The Life and Times of Marsha P. Johnson, Michael Kasino (2012)

Sappho: Love & Life on Lesbos with Margaret Mountford, BBC 4 (2015)

Studio 54, Matt Tyrnauer (2018)

Sylvia Rivera, 'Y'all Better Quiet Down', original authorised video, 1973 Gay Pride Rally, NYC

The Andy Warhol Diaries, Andrew Rossi (2022)

The Celluloid Closet, Rob Epstein and Jeffrey Friedman, based on the book of the same name by Vito Russo (1995)

The Death and Life of Marsha P. Johnson, David France (2017)

The Queen, Frank Simon (1968)

United in Anger: A History of ACT UP, Jim Hubbard and Sarah Schulman (2012)

BOOKS

A Queer History of the United States, Michael Bronski (2011)

Christianity, Social Tolerance, and Homosexuality: Gay People in Western Europe from the Beginning of the Christian Era to the Fourteenth Century, John Boswell (1980)

Encyclopedia of Lesbian Histories and Cultures, edited by Bonnie Zimmerman (1999)

Fabulosa! The Story of Polari, Britain's Secret Gay Language, Paul Baker (2019)

Forbidden Friendships: Homosexuality and Male Culture in Renaissance Florence, Michael Rocke (1998)

Gay Berlin: Birthplace of a Modern Identity, Robert Beachy (2014)

Gay New York: Gender, Urban Culture, and the Making of the Gay Male World, 1890–1940, George Chauncey (1994)

General History of the Pyrates, Daniel Defoe (1724)

Governing Gender and Sexuality in Colonial India: The Hijra, c. 1850–1900, Jessica Hinchy (2019)

Homintern: How Gay Culture Liberated the Modern World, Gregory Woods (2016)

Let the Record Show: A Political History of ACT UP, New York, 1987–1993, Sarah Schulman (2021)

Living Out Loud: A History of Gay and Lesbian Activism in Australia, Graham Willett (2000)

No Modernism Without Lesbians, Diana Souhami (2020)

Passions of the Cut Sleeve: The Male Homosexual Tradition in China, Bret Hinsch (1992)

Queer: A Collection of LGBTQ Writing from Ancient Times to Yesterday, edited by Frank Wynne (2021)

The Forbidden Rumi, translated by Nevit O Ergin and Will Johnson (2006)

The Public Universal Friend: Jemima Wilkinson and Religious Enthusiasm in Revolutionary America, Paul Benjamin Moyer (2015)

The Stonewall Reader, edited by New York Public Library and Jason Baumann (2019)

The Symposium, Plato, translated by Christopher Gill (2003 edition)

Transgender History, Susan Stryker (2008)

Transgender Liberation: A Movement Whose Time Has Come, Leslie Feinberg (1992)

Transgender Warriors: Making History from Joan of Arc to Dennis Rodman, Leslie Feinberg (1996)

Tritiya-Prakriti: People of the Third Sex: Understanding Homosexuality, Transgender Identity and Intersex Conditions Through Hinduism, Amara Das Wilhelm (2008)

Turn the Beat Around: The Secret History of Disco, Peter Shapiro (2005)

We Are Everywhere: Protest, Power and Pride in the History of Queer Liberation, Mathew Reimer and Leighton Brown (2019)

What's Your Pronoun?: Beyond He & She, Dennis Baron (He/Him/His) (2020)

PODCASTS

'Everything You Wanted to Know About Ancient Greece but Were Afraid to Ask', parts 1 and 2, History Extra (2020)

'The Reformation', History Extra (2017)

'They Don't Say Our Names Enough', Code Switch (2020)

'The Stonewall Uprising', You're Wrong About (2019)

Image Credits

Acknowledgements

This book was written on the unceded lands belonging to the Wurundjeri and Boonwurrung peoples of the Kulin Nation. I acknowledge the history of the oldest living cultures in the world and pay my respects to all Aboriginal and Torres Strait Islander peoples reading this book and their Elders and Ancestors. This is, was and will always be Aboriginal land.

This book is a culmination of the love and care of so many individuals.

Thank you to Alice Hardie-Grant for taking a chance on this book. To Emily Hart for taking me under your wing and shepherding this book into the very best version of itself, and for reminding me that we need to have some confidence in bringing Australian stories into global history. To Vanessa Lanaway for helping me make these stories shine and encouraging me to add in humour – something so crucial to our community.

Thank you to Michelle Pereira for your illustrations which are like a window into the past. I love them. And to George Saad, whose design sensibilities have made a patchwork of old images feel connected, and for dealing with the fact I wrote more than we first thought.

Merci, merci, merci to Nadine Al Samman for bringing your insight, research and the MENA perspective to this book. It's that much better for it. Thank you to Rowdie Walden for reading these chapters through First Nations eyes and helping ensure the Indigenous experiences contained within them are truthfully represented.

To Nick Henderson and the Australian Queer Archives for being so generous with your time, knowledge and meticulously maintained collection. To Michael Bronski for taking the time to reply to my email and gifting me a deeper understanding of Marsha and Sylvia.

To Garry Wotherspoon for talking to me about your life as a gay man in Australia in the 70s and 80s. To Diane Minnis and Ken Davis for always answering my questions and inviting me to talk with you about history, or as you call it, gossip. And to all the 78ers, none of us will ever be able to thank you enough for fighting back against the police on 24 June 1978.

To my grandmother Elaine who passed away while this book was being written, thank you for sharing your love of art, history and culture with me. There were so many questions I wish I had asked you, but thank you to my uncles Graeme and Larry, as well as my mother, Robyn, for filling in the blanks.

Rainbow History Class wouldn't exist without Jamie Searle backing the idea, or without Rudy Jean Rigg and all our substitute teachers bringing it to life. To the entire Snack Drawer team for putting your passion and care into this project – it is what it is because of you.

I know we are all so grateful to everyone that follows us, comments and shares our content on social media. Especially to our first followers on TikTok – thank you for being early to class.

Even with everyone I have mentioned, the book wouldn't have made it to print without the support of my family, who brought me coffee and cake and let me take over their living room; friends, who read drafts and offered their thoughts and advice; and finally, my partner in this army of lovers, Hannah Elizabeth Butterworth – thank you for fighting by my side.

Index

Abbasid Caliphate 42, 46
Abram (Abraham) 14–15
Achilles 22–3
Ai, Emperor 28–9
AIDS 171–86
    AIDS Coalition to
    Unleash Power (ACT
    UP) 176–8, 184–6
Alice Springs 132
An Army of Lovers Cannot
    Lose 4, 206
Ancient civilisations 10–35
    China 28–9
    Byzantine Empire 34,
    38–9
    Egypt 12
    Greece 17, 26, 42
    Roman Empire 30–5
    Siwi 14
Antinous 31, 47
Antoinette, Marie 77–8
Antoninus 33
Anything that Moves 192
Archaic Era 21
Aristophanes 25
Arondeus, Willem 130
aversion therapy 155
AZT 176–7

Babylon 14
Baker, Josephine 95
Bay Area Bisexual Network
    192
Bentley, Gladys 105
bisexuality 192–5
    The Bisexual Manifesto
    192, 195
    'uranodionism' 91
    #StillBisexual 194
Black Queer culture 105–7
    Black Power movement
    149
    see also house balls,
    Voguing
Blood Sisters 174
bottom shaming 30
Bowie, David 162, 163

Brown, Rita Mae 150
Buggery Act 1533 52, 68,
    78

Caesar, Julius 30
camp culture 103, 106
Campaign Against Moral
    Persecution (CAMP)
    155
Cannistraci, Lisa 144, 145
Caprotti, Gian Giacomo
    (Salaí) 49
Christianity *see* religion
'Christopher Street
    Liberation Day' 146, *see
    also* Pride
Christopher Street Pier
    148, 153
Class S 109–10
Cold War 131–2
colonisation 58–72, 196
'coming out' 104
Constantine, Emperor 34
Continental Baths 161
COVID-19 172, 175
Cubbyhole 145

da Vinci, Leonardo 48–9
dandy culture 85
Daughters of Bilitis 141–2
decolonisation 72
DeLarverié, Storme 143–5
Dietrich, Marlene 116–17
disco 161–2
Dong Xian 28–9
'Don't Ask, Don't Tell' 136
Douglas, John 82–3
Dracula's Daughter (1936)
    120–1
drag 103, 147, 162–3

Elagabalus, Emperor 33
epidemiology 173
Executive Order 10450
    133–4, 136

Fairies Ball 106
Fanny and Stella 79–80
Feinberg, Leslie 196–8, 201
feminism 149–50, 193, 201
French Revolution (1791) 78
Friedan, Betty 149
friends of Dorothy 119, 135
Garland, Judy 119
gay
    Gay Activists Alliance
    (GAA) 150
    bars 95
    Gay Liberation Front
    146, 149–50
    'the gay plague' 171
    'gay-related
    immunodeficiency'
    (GRID) 171
    see also homosexuality,
    queer
gender
    affirmation surgery 96
    characterisation 94
    in Indigenous cultures
    59–61, 64, 68
    in Shakespeare 53–4
    see also pronouns,
    transgender
Germany 88–9, 97, 131,
    123–30
Girl in Red 76
Gomorrah 16
Great Depression 115
Greenwich Village 101, 142,
    143
Grindr 200

Hadrian, Emperor 31, 47
Hall, Radclyffe 108, 111
Hamilton Lodge 106
Haring, Keith 181, 182–3
Harlem Renaissance 105–6
Hathaway, Anne 54
Hatshepsut 13
Hays Code 118, 121
Hegazi, Sarah 203–5

Henry VIII, King 51–2
Hirschfeld, Magnus 85,
    92–4, 96–7
Hitchcock, Alfred 121
Hitler, Adolf 123
Hollywood 114–22
homophile movement 141–2
homosensuality 43
homosexuality 6, 11–12,
    92, 155
house balls 163–4
    House of LaBeija 163
    House of Ninja 166
    House of Xtravaganza
    167
Howard, Brenda 192–4
Human Rights Commission
    143

The Iliad by Homer 21–3
India 68
Indigenous cultures 59–62,
    68
Institute for Sexual Science
    96–7
internet 199–205
    dating sites 200
Islamic Golden Age 42,
    43, 46

Jewel Box Revue 145
John, Elton 162, 163
John the Baptist 48–9
Johnson, Marsha P 147–8,
    153
Julius' bar 142–3
Justinian I, Emperor 34

Kaposi's sarcoma 171
Kertbeny, Karl Maria 92
Khnumhotep 11–12
King, Martin Luther (Jnr)
    141
Knights Templar 40–1
Kramer, Larry 176–7

LaBeija, Crystal 163
LaBeija, Lottie 163
LaBeija Ball 163
Labouchere Amendment
    80, 81
lavender marriages 119
Lavender Menace 149–50
Lavender Scare 133–4
lesbian 80–1, 107–10, 121,
    127, 132, 149–50, 195,
    154–5, 174
    bars 95–6, 145
    Lesbian Feminist
    Liberation 150
    'lesbian chic' 195
    'Radicalesbians' 150
    see also Sappho
Lesbos 18–20
Leuctra, Battle of 4
the Levant 14
LGBTQ+ acronym 5, 174,
    193
lhamana 60
Lot 16, 42

Madonna 167, 181
Manslaughter (1922) 115
Mashrou' Leila 203, 204
masquerade balls 103,
    105–6, see also drag,
    house balls
Matamba 63
matelotage 66–7
Mattachine Society 141–2
McCarthy, Sen. Joe 133
Medieval Period 42
Mercury, Freddie 162, 163
#metoo 117
Michelangelo 47, 94, 162
Minnelli, Vincente 119
Monma Chiyo 110

National Institute of Health
    (NIH) 177
National Organization
    for Women Second
    Congress to Unite
    Women 149
Naval Investigative Unit
    (NIS) 135–6
Nazi Party 97, 123, 126–30
Ndongo 63
Nelson, Larry 194
Newton, Huey P 149
Niankhkhnum 11–12
Ninja, Willi 164–6
Nobuko Yoshiya 109,
    109–10
Nzinga, Ana 63–4

Obama, President Barack
    136
Obscene Publications Act
    (1857) 111

Pansy Craze 107
Paragraph 175 89, 93, 96,
    127, 131
Paris Is Burning (1991) 166
'passion of the cut sleeve'
    28–9
Patroclus 22–3
pederasty 26–7, 31, 46, 49
Piaf, Edith 117
pirates 65–7
Plato 24, 42
pneumocystis carini
    pneumonia (PCP) 171
Polari 102
police 141, 143, 146, 156
    Office of the Night 46–7
de Polignac, Duchess 77,
    78
Pride
    celebrations 140, 146,
    156
    'pride' 193
    Progress Pride Flag
    202

pronouns 144–5
  neo-pronouns 197–8
  'they' 201
psychosurgery 155
Public Universal Friend
  70–1

Queen Christina (1933) 115
queer 5, 19–1
  coding 118, 120–2
  culture 162, 167, 190–1,
  199
  languages 101–3
  *Queer Eye for the
  Straight Guy* 102
  Queer Nation 191
  Queers Read This!
  190–1

Rainbow Flag 202
Red Scare 133–4
religion 34, 38–55
  Book of Genesis 16–17
  Book of Leviticus 17
  Catholic Church 39, 46,
  118, 131
  Church of England 51–2
  Hinduism 68
  Islam 42–45
  Judaism 127–8, 193, 196
  Lutherism 51
  Old Testament 14–17
  Protestantism 51
  Puritans 52, 53–4, 69
  Quakers 69–71
  the Reformation 51–2
the Renaissance 46–9
Rivera, Sylvia 152–3
Roberts, Capt.
  Bartholomew 67
Rumi, Jalāl al-Din 44–5

Sackville-West, Vita 111
Sacred Bande of Thebes 4
Sailor Moon 110
Sapphic Craze 107

Sappho 18–19, 21, 94
Scientific-Humanitarian
  Committee 93
Section 377 68
Sewing Circle 117
Shakespeare, William 23,
  53–4, 94
Sinno, Hamed 203
sip-in 142
Sisters of Perpetual
  Indulgence 179–80
slavery 62–4, 66, 70–1
Smith, Gwendolyn 199
social media 200, 202
Society of Universal Friends
  71
Socrates 24, 26, 94
Sodom 16, 42, 51
sodomy 16, 39, 52
The Song of Achilles by
  Madeline Miller 23
Stalag 383 129
State Liquor Authority (US)
  141, 143
Stone Butch Blues by Leslie
  Feinberg 197
Stonewall Uprising 143,
  146, 148
'Storm the NIH' protest 178
Studio 54 161–2, 163
Sydney Mardi Gras 155–7
The Symposium by Plato
  23–6, 46

Al Tabrizi, Shams 45
Teena, Brandon 198
The Celluloid Closet (1995)
  122
The Well of Loneliness by
  Radclyffe Hall 108, 111
The Wizard of Oz (1939)
  119
Theodosius, Emperor 34
TikTok 202
transgender 13, 33, 90, 94,
  96–7, 101, 166, 196–200
  Remembering Our Dead

project 199
Street Transvestite
  Action Revolutionaries
  (STAR) 153
'transexual' 196
Transexual Menace 198
Transgender
  Community Forum 199
  Transgender Day of
  Remembrance 199
'transvestites' 96, 196
Trojan War 21–3

Ulrichs, Karl Heinrich 90–2,
  94, 199
uranic attraction 90–2

Victoria, Queen 80
Vincenco, Una 108
Vinceti, Silvano 49
Voguing 164–165

Warhol, Andy 161, 163
We'wha 60
Wilchins, Riki 198
Wilde, Oscar 81–5, 94,
  100–1
Wilkinson, Jemima *see*
  Public Universal Friend
Wilson, George 67
Wings (1927) 115
'Woman-identified Woman'
  150
women's suffrage 107
Woolf, Virginia 111
World War I 107
World War II 126–30

Yaneura no Nishojo by
  Nobuko Yoshiya 109–10
Yuri 110

zines 191, 195, 199
Zuni people 60

Published in 2023 by Hardie Grant Books, an imprint of Hardie Grant Publishing

Hardie Grant Books (Melbourne)
Wurundjeri Country
Building 1, 658 Church Street
Richmond, Victoria 3121

Hardie Grant Books (London)
5th & 6th Floors
52–54 Southwark Street
London SE1 1UN

hardiegrant.com/au/books

Hardie Grant acknowledges the Traditional Owners of the country on which we work, the Wurundjeri people of the Kulin nation and the Gadigal people of the Eora nation, and recognises their continuing connection to the land, waters and culture. We pay our respects to their Elders past and present.

A catalogue record for this
book is available from the
NATIONAL LIBRARY OF AUSTRALIA   National Library of Australia

Rainbow History Class
ISBN 978 1 74379 834 8

10 9 8 7 6 5 4 3 2 1

Every effort has been made to identify copyright holders and obtain their permission. Notification of any corrections would be greatly appreciated.

Design by George Saad
Colour reproduction by Splitting Image Colour Studio
Printed in China by Leo Paper Products LTD.

The paper this book is printed on is from FSC®-certified forests and other sources. FSC® promotes environmentally responsible, socially beneficial and economically viable management of the world's forests.